English Olympiad

Highly useful for all school students participating in Various Olympiads & Competitions

Series Editor Keshav Mohan

Authors Vinay Sharma & Shubhash

Class 5

ARIHANT PRAKASHAN, MEERUT

ARIHANT PRAKASHAN, MEERUT

卐 Administrative & Production Offices

Corporate Office	'Ramchhaya' 4577/15, Agarwal Road, Darya Ganj New Delhi -110002 Tele: 011- 47630600, 43518550; Fax: 011- 23280316
Head Office	Kalindi, TP Nagar, Meerut (UP) - 250002 Tele: 0121-2401479, 2512970, 4004199; Fax: 0121-2401648

All disputes subject to Meerut (UP) jurisdiction only.

卐 Sales & Support Offices

Agra, Ahmedabad, Bengaluru, Bhubaneswar, Bareilly, Chennai, Delhi, Guwahati, Haldwani, Hyderabad, Jaipur, Jalandhar, Jhansi, Kolkata, Kota, Lucknow, Meerut, Nagpur & Pune

卐 ISBN 978-93-5251-198-3

卐 Price ₹65

Typeset by Arihant DTP Unit at Meerut
Printed & Bound by Arihant Publications (I) Ltd. (Press Unit)

Production Team

Publishing Manager	Mahendra Singh Rawat	*Page Layouting*	Bhaskar Rana
Project Head	Mona Yadav	*DTP Operator*	Naveen
Project Coordinator	Priyanka	*Cover Designer*	Syed Darin Zaidi
Proof Reader	Anu Priya, Hareem Khan	*Inner Designer*	Deepak Kumar

For further information about the products from Arihant
log on to www.arihantbooks.com or email to info@arihantbooks.com

Preface

English Olympiad Series for Class 2nd -10th is a series of books which will challenge the young inquisitive minds by the non-routine and exciting Questions on the use of English.

The main purpose of this series is to make the students ready for competitive exams, as English Language is an integral section of almost all competitive examinations. All the questions given in this series are objective in nature so they will provide students a feel of competitive examinations as school/board exams are of qualifying nature but not competitive, which mainly have objective questions.

- **Need of Olympiad Series**
  This series helps students who are willing to sharpen their proficiency in the field of English language. Unlike typical assessment books, which emphasise on drilling practice, the focus of this series is on practising problem solving techniques. It will help the students use the concepts they have learnt to discover that they can actually solve questions.

- **Development of Communication Skills**
  Application based questions given in this series will help students to attain a deeper understanding of different concepts of English Language through which students will be able to imbibe more effective communication skills in themselves.

- **Complement Your School Studies**
  This series complements the additional preparation needs of students for regular school/board exams. By learning English effectively, students will not only be able to perform well in English language exam but also they will perform better in Science/Social Science/Mathematics where medium to write the answer is English. Along with, it will also address all the requirements of the students who are approaching National/State level Olympiads.

I shall welcome criticism from the students, teachers, educators and parents. I shall also like to hear from all of you about errors and shortcomings which may have remained in this edition and the suggestions for their improvement in the next edition.

Editor

Contents

Nouns

A noun is the name of a person, place, thing or quality.

e.g. Dr. Ashish is a famous neurosurgeon.
Our Prime Minister recently visited Bangladesh.

In the above examples, 'Dr. Ashish', 'neurosurgeon', 'Prime Minister' and 'Bangladesh' are nouns.

Types of Noun

There are five types of noun:

1. **Proper Nouns** These nouns refer to the specific name of a person, place or thing. Proper nouns begin with capital letters and are generally singular in nature.
   e.g. Mumbai, Taj Mahal, Ram etc.
2. **Common Nouns** These are used in general for people, place, things or ideas of the same class. It is a name given in common to each member or unit of the class.
   e.g. soldier, children, books etc.
3. **Collective Nouns** These nouns are the names of a group or collection of persons or things taken together and spoken of as a whole.
   e.g. army, committee, bunch etc.
4. **Abstract Nouns** These nouns refer to the name of a quality, action or state or feeling that cannot be seen or touched.
   e.g. happiness, love, honesty etc.
5. **Material Nouns** These nouns are the names of matter or substance of which things are made. These nouns cannot be counted.
   e.g. coal, gold, water etc.

Another classification of noun are as follow:

1. **Countable Nouns** These are the names of objects, people etc., that we can count.
   e.g. book, pen, apple, sister etc.
2. **Uncountable Nouns** These are the names of things which we cannot count.
   e.g. milk, oil, sugar etc.
   Countable nouns may have plural forms while uncountable nouns not; we may say books or chairs, but we cannot say milks or waters.

Let's Practice

Directions (Q. Nos. 1-5) Choose the appropriate noun from the options given below to complete the sentences.

1. The .... still has not taken our order.
(a) porter (b) manager
(c) waiter (d) shopkeeper

2. The Nile is the longest of all the ....
(a) lakes (b) oceans
(c) seas (d) rivers

3. I do not travel with much ....
(a) furniture (b) food
(c) work (d) luggage

4. .... is on the banks of river Hooghly.
(a) Kelkata (b) Kolkata
(c) Calcutta (d) None of these

5. Our .... fought with great courage during the Kargil War.
(a) men (b) soldiers
(c) politicians (d) students

Directions (Q. Nos. 6-10) Which type of noun the underlined word is?

6. Solomon was the wisest of all kings.
(a) Common noun (b) Proper noun
(c) Abstract noun (d) Collective noun

7. The soldiers were rewarded for their bravery.
(a) Common noun
(b) Proper noun
(c) Abstract noun
(d) Material noun

8. The French army was defeated at Waterloo.
(a) Common noun
(b) Collective noun
(c) Proper noun
(d) Abstract noun

9. Gold is a precious metal.
(a) Proper noun (b) Common noun
(c) Abstract noun (d) Material noun

10. Banana is a very nutritious fruit.
(a) Proper noun
(b) Common noun
(c) Collective noun
(d) Abstract noun

Directions (Q. Nos. 11-15) Choose the correct corresponding noun of the given words.

11. Succeed
(a) Succeeded (b) Success
(c) Succession (d) Succeeding

12. Write
(a) Writing (b) Written (c) Writer (d) Wrote

13. Laugh
(a) Laughter (b) Laughed
(c) Laughingly (d) Laughing

14. Vacant
(a) Vacated (b) Vacate
(c) Vacancy (d) Vacantly

15. Know
(a) Knew (b) Known
(c) Knowledge (d) Knowing

Directions (Q. Nos. 16-17) Match the words in List I with their appropriate options in List II.

16.

	List I (Word)		List II (Collective Noun)
A.	Keys	1.	Committee
B.	Flowers	2.	Bunch
C.	Members	3.	Herd
D.	Cattle	4.	Bouquet

Codes

	A	B	C	D		A	B	C	D
(a)	4	1	2	3	(b)	2	4	1	3
(c)	1	3	2	4	(d)	3	4	2	1

17.

	List I (Word)		List II (Types of Noun)
A.	Jawaharlal Nehru	1.	Collective
B.	Fleet	2.	Common
C.	Chairs	3.	Abstract
D.	Happiness	4.	Proper

Codes

	A	B	C	D		A	B	C	D
(a)	2	1	3	4	(b)	4	1	2	3
(c)	4	3	2	1	(d)	3	2	1	4

18. The noun which is used both as singular and plural.
(a) Tie (b) Coat
(c) Shirt (d) Trousers

19. Choose correct list of plural nouns.
(a) Fan, sheep, table, boys
(b) Sheep, oxen, books, mice
(c) Bag, watch, sheep, bottles
(d) Knife, books, chairs, bottles

20. Which of the following is not a singular noun?
(a) Toe (b) Ankle (c) Knee (d) Feet

Directions (Q. Nos. 21-24) Choose the correct abstract noun from the given options.

21. (a) Honest (b) Honestly
(c) Honestness (d) Honesty

22. (a) Good (b) Goodness
(c) Goodie (d) Good deed

23. (a) Slave (b) Slaver
(c) Slavery (d) Slaved

24. (a) Strong (b) Strongest
(c) Stronger (d) Strength

Directions (Q. Nos. 25-28) Choose the correct collective noun from the given options.

25. (a) Flower (b) Rose
(c) Bouquet (d) Garden

26. (a) Parent (b) Family
(c) Brother (d) Sister

27. (a) Harbour (b) Ship
(c) Sailor (d) Fleet

28. (a) Gun (b) Soldier
(c) War (d) Army

Directions (Q. Nos. 29-31) Choose the correct sentence of the questions.

29. Why is Sudha packing her bag?
(a) She is going to her uncle's place for christmas Holidays.
(b) She is going to her Uncle's place for christmas Holidays.
(c) She is going to her uncle's place for Christmas Holidays.
(d) She is going to her uncle's place for Christmas holidays.

30. Which is the tallest building in the world?
(a) The tallest building in the world is the burj khalifa in Dubai.
(b) The tallest building in the world is the Burj khalifa in Dubai.
(c) The tallest building in the world is the burj khalifa in dubai.
(d) None of the above

31. Where are you going in vacation?
(a) We are going to shimla in summer holidays.
(b) We are going to Shimla in summer holidays.
(c) We are going to Shimla in summer Holidays.
(d) None of the above

Directions (Q. Nos. 32-36) Find the odd one out from the given options.

32. (a) Nightingale (b) Sparrow
(c) Maina (d) Bird

33. (a) Gold (b) Silver (c) Irony (d) Iron

34. (a) Advise (b) Happiness
(c) Kindness (d) Obedience

35. (a) Principal (b) Teacher (c) Class (d) Student

36. (a) Bundle (b) Bunch (c) Bouquet (d) Bark

Directions (Q. Nos. 37-41) Read the passage carefully and answer the questions that follow.

Jane Goodall is a remarkable woman who has led an extraordinary life. She was born in London on 3rd April, 1934. When Jane was a child, she liked watching the animals and birds in her garden, but she dreamed of travelling to Africa to observe exotic animals in their natural habitat. Jane became famous for her amazing work as an expert on the behaviour of chimpanzee in Tanzania.

37. In the first line of the passage, the underlined word is a ....

(a) Common noun (b) Proper noun
(c) Collective noun (d) Abstract noun

38. In the third sentence of the passage, which of the following is a proper noun?

(a) Child (b) Garden
(c) Jane (d) Birds

39. Choose the correct type of noun for the underlined words given in the third sentence of the passage.

(a) Abstract noun (b) Proper noun
(c) Common noun (d) Collective noun

40. Which type of noun is the word 'habitat' in the passage?

(a) Common noun (b) Abstract noun
(c) Collective noun (d) Proper noun

41. Which noun has been used in plural form in the last sentence of the passage?

(a) Expert (b) Chimpanzee
(c) Tanzania (d) Behaviour

Directions (Q. Nos. 42-50) Read the passage given below and fill in the blanks with the most suitable option.

Madagascar is a fairly large .....(42)..... in the Indian ......(43)....... . It has many dense .....(44)..... full of poisonous ....(45)...... and a large variety of wild ......(46)..... . There are a number of hills and deep ...... (47)..... . It is a backward country and far behind modern ..... (48)..... . Only a few .....(49)..... visit this place due to its unfavourable geographical location. The new name of this ...... (50) ..... is Malagasy Republic.

42. (a) area (b) sea (c) land (d) island

43. (a) continent (b) ocean
(c) peninsula (d) island

44. (a) tracts (b) forests
(c) animals (d) places

45. (a) animals (b) snakes
(c) wildlife (d) people

46. (a) places (b) people
(c) animals (d) trees

47. (a) seas (b) rivers
(c) valleys (d) plateaus

48. (a) civilisation (b) country
(c) world (d) land

49. (a) children (b) sailors
(c) tourists (d) adventurists

50. (a) continent (b) country
(c) colony (d) national

Pronouns

A pronoun is a word that refers to a noun already mentioned in a sentence. It is used to avoid repetition of noun in a sentence.

e.g. Ram did not go to school as 'he' was not well.

In the sentence above, 'he' is used in place of 'Ram' to avoid repetition of the word 'Ram'.

Some examples of pronouns are *I, we, you, they, it, he, she, who, myself, these, nothing, mine* etc.

Types of Pronoun

There are seven types of pronoun :

1. **Personal Pronouns** They describe a particular person, thing or group. These pronouns describe the person speaking (I, me, we, us), the person spoken to (you) or the person or thing spoken about (he, she, it, they, him, her, them).
2. **Possessive Pronouns** These pronouns are used to show ownership or close possession of a thing/person to another thing/person.

   e.g. *yours, mine, his, her(s), ours* etc.
3. **Reflexive Pronouns** These pronouns describe a noun when a subject's action affects the subject itself.

   e.g. *himself, herself, yourself, themselves, ourselves* etc.
4. **Relative Pronouns** These pronouns join two statements or sentences.

   e.g. who, whom, whose, which etc.
5. **Demonstrative Pronouns** These pronouns point to a thing or things.

   e.g. *this, that, these, those, none* and *neither*.
6. **Indefinite Pronouns** These pronouns are used for non-specific things.

   e.g. *all, some, any, several, anyone, nobody, nothing, each, every, both, few, none, either* etc.
7. **Interrogative Pronouns** These pronouns are used in forming questions.

   e.g. *what, who, which, where, how* etc.

Let's Practice

Directions (Q. Nos. 1-15) Fill in the blanks by choosing the correct option.

1. Leena and Payal are very excited because .... are going to Disneyland.
(a) that (b) those
(c) there (d) they

2. Mahima and Kajal are doctors and .... profession is very noble.
(a) her (b) hers (c) them (d) their

3. .... wants to go to a hill station in summer.
(a) Everyone (b) Someone
(c) Anyone (d) No one

4. One should always keep .... word.
(a) his (b) her
(c) their (d) All of these

5. .... Suresh and Mayank had been ex-monitors of my class.
(a) They (b) Them (c) Both (d) Those

6. After accident, Sanjeev is unable to move .... legs.
(a) those (b) his (c) its (d) himself

7. My sister and .... went to watch a movie yesterday.
(a) me (b) my (c) I (d) her

8. Would you please call ....?
(a) herself (b) hers
(c) both (a) and (b) (d) None of these

9. "The children ....work is neat and finished in time will get two marks extra," said the teacher.
(a) which (b) whose (c) that (d) where

10. Did you draw this picture............?
(a) myself (b) itself
(c) yourself (d) himself

11. Neha is the girl .... laptop was stolen today.
(a) her (b) hers (c) whose (d) whom

12. This is the car .... had an accident
(a) who (b) which (c) whose (d) whom

13. Shishir is boy .... father works at SBI.
(a) who (b) whose (c) whom (d) which

14. Karuna and Jyoti have not met .... for a long time.
(a) herself (b) themself
(c) themselves (d) each other

15. Students helped .... with their reports.
(a) each other (b) himself
(c) herself (d) themselves

Directions (Q. Nos. 16-21) Which type of pronoun the underlined word is?

16. <u>He</u> wants to start his own business.
(a) Possessive (b) Personal
(c) Reflexive (d) Indefinite

17. <u>Why</u> are you shouting at servants?
(a) Personal (b) Relative
(c) Demonstrative (d) Interrogative

18. I can't believe its finally <u>ours</u>.
(a) Reflexive (b) Possessive
(c) Indefinite (d) Interrogative

19. She wants to do everything <u>herself</u>.
(a) Possessive (b) Reflexive
(c) Personal (d) Demonstrative

20. <u>Those</u> are my tea estates.
(a) Interrogative (b) Demonstrative
(c) Relative (d) Reflexive

21. The girl <u>who</u> usually keeps quiet is making lots of noise.
(a) Personal (b) Reflexive
(c) Relative (d) Interrogative

Directions (Q. Nos. 22-25) Find the odd one out.

22. (a) My (b) Her
(c) They (d) This

23. (a) Which (b) What
(c) Mine (d) Where

24. (a) Ourselves (b) Those
(c) Myself (d) Themselves

25. (a) None (b) Anybody
(c) Everyone (d) She

Directions (Q. Nos. 26-28) Replace the underlined words with the suitable pronoun from the options given below.

26. Probably the captain doesn't expect John and Parikh to finish the work in time.
(a) we (b) us (c) them (d) they

27. My family and I are going on a vacation to Singapore.
(a) We (b) Us
(c) Our (d) Ourselves

28. We had invited the guests this morning only.
(a) us (b) we (c) them (d) those

Directions (Q. Nos. 29-32) Find the category of pronoun.

29. Which option shows personal pronouns?
(a) this, that, those, these
(b) what, why, where, how
(c) I, he, she, you, we
(d) everybody, nobody, somebody, none

30. Which option shows possessive pronouns?
(a) myself, herself, himself, themselves
(b) mine, hers, yours, ours
(c) it, he, she, they
(d) where, why, how

31. Which option shows reflexive pronouns?
(a) each other, one another, all
(b) herself, myself, yourself, ourselves
(c) we, it, she, you
(d) that, those, these, this

32. Which option shows indefinite pronouns?
(a) himself, yourself, herself
(b) mine, hers, their, yours
(c) all, some, any, nobody, each
(d) this, that, those, these

Directions (Q. Nos. 33-34) Match List I with List II and choose the correct option.

33.

	List I		List II
A.	Bring me the file	1.	Who lives in Lucknow.
B.	I have a brother	2.	Whose father is in army.
C.	He is Shastri	3.	Which is on the table.
D.	The boys	4.	Who shouted in the class were punished.

Codes

	A	B	C	D		A	B	C	D
(a)	2	4	1	3	(b)	3	4	1	2
(c)	4	3	1	2	(d)	3	2	1	4

34.

	List I		List II
A.	As for myself, I prefer to let people make up	1.	his lunch.
B.	Either John or Harry forgot to take	2.	their bank accounts.
C.	The cat itself	3.	their minds.
D.	The politicians are busy in filling	4.	decided to jump.

Codes

	A	B	C	D		A	B	C	D
(a)	2	3	1	4	(b)	4	1	2	3
(c)	3	2	1	4	(d)	3	1	4	2

Directions (Q. Nos. 35-38) Fill the blanks with correct pronouns to make the sentence meaningful.

35. The old woman lived alone with ....to look after ....
(a) someone/her (b) no one/her
(c) anyone/herself (d)anyone/she's

36. A baby learns the meaning of words as .... are spoken and later uses ....in sentences.
(a) their/they (b) they/themselves
(c) they/them (d) they/it

37. ....two rings on my little finger belonged to ....grandmother.
(a) These/my (b) Those/me
(c) The/myself (d) This/my

38. Some of these clothes are ....and the rest of ....are mine.
(a) ours/they (b) yours/them
(c) hers/their (d) mine/them

Directions (Q. Nos. 39-43) Read the passage carefully and fill in the blanks with correct pronouns.

Marie Curie was born in 1867 in Warsaw, Poland. ......(39)...... is one of the greatest scientists ever to have lived. She was a pioneer in the field of radioactivity and discovered the element radium. ......(40)...... father was a Mathematics and Physics teacher and was a big influence on Marie. From an early age, Marie was an exceptional student ......(41)....... . She met her future husband Pierre Curie at the university. ......(42)...... considered Marie to be a genius and wished her to work with him. They got married and spent most of ......(43)...... time together in their laboratory. Their research led to the discovery of radium for which they were honoured with the Nobel Prize in 1903.

39. (a) Herself (b) Hers (c) She (d) Her

40. (a) Their (b) Her (c) Herself (d) Hers

41. (a) itself (b) himself (c) yourself (d) herself

42. (a) We (b) They (c) Us (d) He

43. (a) her (b) their (c) our (d) your

Directions (Q. Nos. 44-48) Read the passage carefully and answer the questions that follow.

All our surroundings including air, water, soil, trees and animals make up our environment. When the normal relations among *these* elements of nature are disturbed, the ecological balance is hampered and it is called environmental pollution. The impact of environment pollution is very dangerous. The smoke from factories and other vehicles contains harmful substances like carbon monoxide and sulphur dioxide. These hamper the cleanliness of the air. Mills and factories set up on river banks let out chemical wastes into the river water.

When people drink this water or take a bath in the polluted water, they are attacked with stomach and skin diseases.

Environmental pollution may be controlled by taking various measures. We may increase afforestation. Laws should be passed to prevent factories from dumping wastes. Moreover, every conscious individual and institution should come forward to solve this problem for the sake of our existence.

44. Find the pronouns in the first sentence of the passage.
(a) Surroundings (b) All
(c) Our (d) Air

45. What type of pronoun is the *underlined* word in second sentence of the paragraph?
(a) Personal pronoun
(b) Possessive pronoun
(c) Demonstrative pronoun
(d) Interrogative pronoun

46. The underlined word 'these' is used in the passage for
(a) factories
(b) carbon monoxide and sulphur dioxide
(c) smoke
(d) vehicles

47. What will be the possessive pronoun corresponding to the underlined word 'they' in the passage?
(a) Your (b) Their
(c) Mine (d) Its

48. What kind of pronoun is the underlined word 'every'?
(a) Interrogative (b) Reflexive
(c) Indefinite (d) Possessive

Directions (Q. Nos. 49-52) Fill in the blanks in the passage with appropriate reflexive pronouns.

A tom cat heard that there were some hens on a farm who had hurt ......(49)...... . So, he disguised ......(50)...... as a doctor and went there with his bag. He knocked at the coop and said,

"Dear little hens, I have prepared some medicine ......(51)......, it will heal your wounds."

One of the hens cried back, "We can take care of that ......(52)....... . If you will go away from here, we shall soon get well".

49. (a) myself (b) themselves
(c) yourself (d) ourselves

50. (a) itself (b) himself
(c) herself (d) yourself

51. (a) ourselves (b) itself
(c) yourself (d) myself

52. (a) ourselves
(b) yourself
(c) themselves
(d) itself

Articles

An article is a word used with a noun to indicate the type of reference being made by the noun. Article defines a noun as specific or unspecific.

e.g.
- I have a book with me.
- She is eating an ice cream.
- The dress you gave me is really pretty.

  Here, 'a', 'an' and 'the' are articles.

Types of Article

There are two types of article:

1. **Indefinite Article** 'A' and 'An' are indefinite articles which are used with singular nouns.

   e.g. 1. That is a glass. 2. There is an insect under the table.

   Note 1. 'A' is used when the noun begins with a consonant sound.
   2. 'An' is used when the noun begins with a vowel sound.

Use of the Indefinite Articles 'A' and 'An'.

	Usage	Example
A.	With countable nouns that are unspecified (i.e. referred to for the first time)	A girl, a pencil, an orange
B.	When the noun is one of a group	Sarita is a student of Class V-B.
C.	What a person is/what job the person does	Sudhir is a doctor.
D.	Used for meaning 'one'	I'd like an apple, please.
E.	Saying something about all things of that kind	A dog likes to chew bones.
F.	Before collective nouns and some numbers	A bunch of flowers, a shoal of fish, a dozen, a thousand
G.	With nouns to form adverbial phrases of amount, quantity or degree	I feel a bit afraid
H.	With nationalities / religions in the singular	An Indian, a Muslim

2. **Definite Article** 'The' is definite article as it points to a particular object or class. It is used with both singular and plural nouns. It can also be used with countables, like the stars, the table etc, as well as with uncountables, like the milk, the courage, the passion etc.

Uses of Definite Article 'The'

	Usage	Example
A.	Superlatives	Everest is *the* highest mountain in the world.
B.	Nationals of a country	*The* Indians live in India.
C.	Holy books	*The* Mahabharat, *The* Bhagwad Gita
D.	Nature	*The* Earth, *The* Sun
E.	Rivers	*The* Ganges, *The* Thames
F.	Seas and oceans	*The* Indian ocean, *The* Arabian sea
G.	Monuments	*The* Taj Mahal, *The* Red Fort
H.	Important posts	*The* President, *The* Prime Minister

Let's Practice

Directions (Q. Nos. 1-11) Fill in the blanks with suitable article from the options given below.

1. .... Tower of London is .... popular tourist place.

(a) The/a (b) An/the
(c) A/an (d) The/the

2. Where is ...... video game I gave you yesterday?

(a) an (b) a
(c) the (d) No article

3. Binod has .... terrible headache.

(a) an (b) a
(c) the (d) No article

4. Allahabad is situated on the bank of .... Ganga.

(a) an (b) a
(c) the (d) No article

5. There is nothing like staying at ...... home for relaxation.

(a) an (b) a
(c) the (d) No article

6. I watched a magic show two days ago which was .... exciting experience.

(a) the (b) a (c) an (d) No article

7. .... mangoes and .... apples are exported to other countries from India.

(a) A/the (b) The/the
(c) The/a (d) No articles

8. .... Air India has shown signs of improvement.

(a) A (b) An
(c) The (d) No article

9. My mother bought .... expensive saree on Mother's Day.

(a) an (b) a
(c) the (d) No article

10. Look, there is .... little squirrel on this tree!

(a) an (b) the
(c) a (d) No article

11. I hate .... geography and biology. .... only subject I like is English.

(a) the/The (b) No article/The
(c) a/An (d) the/A

Directions (Q. Nos.12-16) Answer the following questions by filling the blanks with the most appropriate article from the given options.

12. What did you get for your birthday?
I got .... lot of good presents.
(a) a (b) the (c) an (d) No article

13. Where are you going for your vacations?
I am going to .... hill station in Himachal Pradesh.
(a) an (b) a (c) the (d) No article

14. Do you think your friend is lying?
No, he is the kind of .... guy who never tells lies.
(a) the (b) an (c) a (d) No article

15. How is your grandfather?
He is .... little sick, but it is nothing serious.
(a) an (b) a (c) the (d) No article

16. Where were you last night? I called you so many times.
Oh sorry, ...yesterday my mobile was off.
(a) the (b) an (c) a (d) No article

Directions (Q. Nos. 17-18) Match List I with List II in order to form meaningful sentences.

17.

	List I		List II
A.	Rebecca works in	1.	an Indian boy.
B.	Mike lives in	2.	hosted by the Bhallas.
C.	Jane wants to marry	3.	a book shop.
D.	I am not attending the party	4.	an old house.

Codes

	A	B	C	D		A	B	C	D
(a)	3	1	2	3	(b)	3	4	1	2
(c)	2	4	1	2	(d)	2	3	4	1

18.

	List I		List II
A.	Do you have .... pen?	1.	an
B.	Is this .... pen given by Mr Singh?	2.	No article
C.	Amit is....... MBA from Rajasthan University.	3.	the
D.	How do I go to .... Lajpat nagar?	4.	a

Codes

	A	B	C	D		A	B	C	D
(a)	2	3	1	4	(b)	4	3	1	2
(c)	3	2	1	4	(d)	2	1	3	4

Directions (Q. Nos. 19-20) Choose the best option with correct use of article(s).

19. 1. Mr Sharma is a best doctor.
2. Mr Sharma is the best doctor.
3. Mr Sharma is an best doctor.
4. Mr Sharma is best doctor.

Codes
(a) Only 1 (b) Only 4
(c) Only 2 (d) Only 3

20. 1. The train stopped at station.
2. The train stopped at a station.
3. The train stopped at the station.
4. The train stopped at an station.

Codes
(a) Only 1 (b) Only 4
(c) Only 2 (d) Only 3

Directions (Q. Nos. 21-36) Fill in the blanks with suitable article in the passage given below from the options given.

I just received a postcard from ...(21)..... Robinsons, a family I met last year. It made me start thinking. When was .... (22)....... last time I actually sent ......(23)...... letter or ......(24)...... postcard to someone? It is strange that ......(25)...... postal services have been part of our daily life for ......(26)...... centuries and suddenly within ..... (27)...... single generation .... (28)...... postal system is on its way to becoming ......(29)..... thing of ......(30)..... past. Today .....(31)..... e-mail is ...... (32)..... far more common way to communicate with .... (33) friends and the family. It is also ......(34)..... faster and a cheaper way to communicate. When I send ......(35)..... e-mail to a friend to a far off country, the friend will receive ......(36)..... e-mail almost immediately.

21. (a) a (b) an (c) the (d) No article

22. (a) a (b) the (c) an (d) No article

23. (a) an (b) the (c) a (d) No article

24. (a) a (b) the (c) an (d) No article

25. (a) an (b) a (c) the (d) No article

26. (a) a (b) an (c) the (d) No article

27. (a) a (b) an (c) the (d) No article

28. (a) a (b) an (c) the (d) No article

29. (a) a (b) the (c) an (d) No article

30. (a) the (b) an (c) a (d) No article

31. (a) the (b) an (c) a (d) No article

32. (a) the (b) an (c) a (d) No article

33. (a) an (b) a (c) the (d) No article

34. (a) an (b) the (c) a (d) No article

35. (a) the (b) an (c) a (d) No article

36. (a) an (b) the (c) a (d) No article

Directions (Q. Nos. 37-40) Read the passage given below and answer the questions that follow.

Fish and Whales are both vertebrates which means they both have backbones. They also live in aquatic environments. Except for a couple of species, whales live only in the ocean water.

Fish however, inhabit both fresh and salt water. Whales are among the largest animals on Earth and some fish can be among the smallest. Whales have a thick layer of fat called blubber under their smooth, almost hairless skin.

This fat helps them to retain their body heat. Fish have very little fat; that is why many fish are prized as food. To keep away from freezing in the cold water, fish blood contains an anti-freeze substance.

37. In third sentence of the passage, the first underlined word is a/an

(a) definite article (b) indefinite article
(c) determiner (d) None of these

38. In third sentence of the passage which is a definite article?

(a) in (b) the (c) ocean (d) only

39. In the fifth sentence, the underlined definite article is used because it can be used ....

(a) to name certain books
(b) before superlatives
(c) before a musical instrument
(d) before the names of rivers

40. In the last sentence of the passage, indefinite article 'an' is used because ....

(a) the word following it is a consonant
(b) the word following it is a word starting with a vowel sound
(c) the word following it is not related to its use
(d) None of the above

Directions (Q. Nos. 41-44) Choose the correct answer of the questions.

41. When is the birthday of your brother?

A. ____________________

(a) Birthday of my brother is in the February.
(b) Birthday of my brother is in February.
(c) The birthday of my brother is in the February.
(d) The birthday of my brother is in a February.

42. How do you go to school?

A. ____________________

(a) I go to school by a bus.
(b) I go to school by the bus.
(c) I go to school by bus.
(d) I go to the school by the bus.

43. When is your father coming back?

A. ____________________

(a) He is coming back on the Monday.
(b) He is coming back on a Monday.
(c) He is coming back on Monday.
(d) None of the above

44. What is this noise?

A. ____________________

(a) I think it is the airplane.
(b) I think it is airplane.
(c) I think it is an airplane.
(d) I think it is a airplane.

Adjectives

Adjectives are words that describe or classify someone or something. They give some information about shape, size, colour, age, origin or any other attribute of things or persons.

e.g. Benjamin is a smart and clever boy.

The form of adjectives never changes i.e. the same adjective is used with singular and plural nouns.

e.g. All boys in this class are smart and clever.

Adjectives appear immediately before noun in a sentence.

e.g. Reeta bought a beautiful dress.

We put an adjective after 'be' in the sentence.

e.g. We are thirsty

We sometimes use verbs such as look, feel, taste, smell etc instead of 'be'.

e.g. You look happy today.

I feel cold.

This cake tastes good.

Generally, adjectives of opposite meaning are formed by adding a prefix such as un, im, in, or dis.

e.g.

Clear	Unclear	Definite	Indefinite
Common	Uncommon	Correct	Incorrect
Certain	Uncertain	Complete	Incomplete
Perfect	Imperfect	Able	Disable
Possible	Impossible	Content	Discontent

Kinds of Adjective

There are five kinds of adjective

1. **Adjective of Quality** This type of adjective shows the quality of a person or a thing.

   e.g. a large city, a foolish crow etc.

2. **Adjective of Quantity** This type of adjective answers the question of how much or how many.

   e.g. 40 oranges, some milk etc.

3. **Demonstrative Adjective** : This type of adjective points out a noun.

   e.g. this boy, these mangoes, that table, etc.

4. **Interrogative Adjectives** This type of adjective is used for asking questions followed by a noun.

   e.g. which book, whose shoes etc.

5. **Numeral Adjective** These adjectives can be further divided into definite numeral, indefinite numeral and distributive numeral.

   e.g. one, two, three, all, many, few, some, each, every, either, neither, etc.

Comparison of Adjectives

There are three degrees of adjectives. They are used to show comparison between two or more persons. In each degree, the adjective changes its form. The three degrees are positive, comparative and superlative.

This can easily be understood by reading the table given below.

Positive	Comparative	Superlative
Clean	Cleaner	Cleanest
Good	Better	Best
Little	Less	Least
Bad	Worse	Worst

e.g. Ramesh is a good student.
Suresh is better than Ramesh.
Suresh is the best student in the class.

The comparative and superlative form of some adjectives are formed by adding **more** or **most** to the positive adjective, respectively.

Let's Practice

Directions (Q. Nos. 1-7) Fill the blanks by choosing suitable adjective from the options given.

1. They live in a .... house.
(a) loveliest (b) lovelier
(c) lovely (d) lovelyful

2. Ramesh is a .... boy.
(a) modester (b) modest
(c) modestest (d) most modest

3. Bina is an .... baby.
(a) adored (b) adore
(c) adorable (d) adoring

4. Gold is ______ than silver.
(a) costly (b) heavy
(c) costlier (d) shiny

5. Sally's watch is .... than years.
(a) expensive (b) more expensive
(c) most expensive (d) None of these

6. English is .... to learn than French.
(a) easy (b) tough (c) difficult (d) easier

7. Parthiv scored the .... marks in the class.
(a) less (b) low (c) little (d) least

Directions (Q. Nos. 8-12) In each of the following questions, identify the kind of adjective that is underlined.

8. There is a sharp increase in the sale of cars from the last month.
(a) Adjective of quantity
(b) Adjective of quality
(c) Definite numeral adjective
(d) Interrogative

9. <u>This</u> quilt is very warm and soft.
(a) Adjective of quantity
(b) Demonstrative adjective
(c) Numeral adjective
(d) Interrogative adjective

10. <u>Every</u> student must finish his homework.
(a) Definite numeral adjective
(b) Adjective of quality
(c) Adjective of quantity
(d) Distributive numeral adjective

11. Did you get <u>any</u> information about reopening of school?
(a) Adjective of number
(b) Adjective of quantity
(c) Indefinite numeral adjective
(d) Demonstrative adjective

12. <u>Whose</u> book is this?
(a) Adjective of quantity
(b) Interrogative adjective
(c) Demonstrative adjective
(d) Numeral adjective

Directions (Q. Nos. 13-15) Choose the appropriate adjective corresponding to the given word.

13. Care
(a) Caring (b) Careful
(c) Carefully (d) Carefulness

14. Talk
(a) Talking (b) Talkative (c) Talkable (d) Talked

15. Cheer
(a) Cheering (b) Cheerful
(c) Cheerfulness (d) Cheered

Directions (Q. Nos. 16-23) Fill in the blanks by choosing the most appropriate degree of adjective.

16. As we hiked up the hill, our steps got ....
(a) short (b) shorter
(c) shortest (d) None of these

17. My sister wants the music to be .... than it is now.
(a) louder (b) loud
(c) loudest (d) None of these

18. There are .... cities in every state and country.
(a) more (b) much
(c) many (d) most

19. Saturday is the most .... day of my weekly routine.
(a) exciting (b) interesting
(c) happening (d) All of these

20. My friend, Jacob was declared the .... sportsman of the school.
(a) least (b) better (c) best (d) good

21. We were very scared when we heard a .... bang.
(a) loudest (b) loud
(c) louder (d) None of these

22. Sarita thinks that the Doremon show is the ....
(a) funnier (b) funny
(c) funniest (d) None of these

23. The people of India are .... than people of any other country.
(a) friendly (b) more friendly
(c) most friendly (d) None of these

Directions (Q. Nos. 24-26) Match items from List I with List II, to form meaningful sentences.

24.

	List I		List II
A.	The criminal was	1.	a left handed batsman.
B.	Our class teacher is	2.	hard working student.
C.	Romal is a	3.	caught red-handed.
D.	Deepa's father is	4.	well-informed about sports.

Codes

	A	B	C	D		A	B	C	D
(a)	3	2	4	1	(b)	2	3	4	1
(c)	3	4	2	1	(d)	1	4	3	2

25.

	List I		List II
A.	Neha's handwriting	1.	is worse than mine.
B.	Sakshi is	2.	more interested in singing than dancing.
C.	She is the	3.	more beautiful than others in the class.
D.	I am	4.	fastest swimmer in the school.

Codes

	A	B	C	D		A	B	C	D
(a)	2	1	4	3	(b)	1	2	3	4
(c)	2	4	3	1	(d)	3	2	1	4

26.

List I	List II
A. Do regular exercise	1. favourite meal.
B. In the Maths unit test	2. heavy rainfall this morning.
C. Breakfast is my	3. I made one careless mistake.
D. The weather forecast said there would be	4. to keep your body healthy.

Codes

	A	B	C	D
(a)	2	3	4	1
(b)	2	1	3	4
(c)	1	3	2	4
(d)	4	3	1	2

Directions (Q. Nos. 27-29) Select the option with the correct use of adjectives.

27. A. He showed concern little for his new teacher.
B. He showed little concern for his new teacher.
C. He showed no concern for his maths.
D. He showed less concern for his maths teacher.

Codes
(a) Option C is correct
(b) Option B is correct
(c) Option B and C are correct
(d) None of the above

28. A. The last news from Myanmar is very disturbing.
B. The latest news from Myanmar is very disturbing.
C. We expect to get the latest updates on the arrival of the monsoon.
D. We expect to get the last update on the arrival of the monsoon.

Codes
(a) B and D are correct (b) A and C are correct
(c) B and C are correct (d) A and D are correct

29. A. I am tired and can't walk any further.
B. I am tired and can't walk any farther.
C. The Vice Principal will act as new Principal until farther orders.
D. The Vice Principal will act as the new principal until further orders.

Codes
(a) Option B and D are correct
(b) Option A and option C are correct
(c) Option A and option D are correct
(d) Option A and B are correct

Directions (Q. Nos. 30-31) Read the following pairs of statements and select correct option.

30. (i) This is the next post office to my house.
(ii) The police station nearest to my house is just 2 kms away.

Codes
(a) Correct/Incorrect (b) Incorrect/Incorrect
(c) Incorrect/Correct (d) Correct/Correct

31. (i) I have an elder sister.
(ii) John is elder than Marc by 3 years.

Codes
(a) Correct/Incorrect (b) Incorrect/Correct
(c) Incorrect/Incorrect (d) Correct/Correct

Directions (Q. Nos. 32-40) Read the letter and fill in the blanks with correct adjective.

15th November, 2014

Dear Dr Harrison,

I would like to write to you a letter of ......(32)...... thanking you for all of the ......(33)...... things you have done for our DAV Middle School in the last one-and-a-half years. You have made an ......(34)...... contribution to our school in such a ......(35)...... time. The whole city was well aware of this when our school was declared the best in academics as well as in sports.

I really enjoy seeing your ......(36)...... face in the morning as I am getting off the bus. I always know when you are unwell or out of town because ......(37)...... are the only days, I do not see you on the sidewalk. The students are really ......(38)...... by the scheduling of lunch-hours as everyone has finished eating by 1:30. I love it when you come to watch our basketball games on Saturday; we all seem to play a little ......(39)......, knowing you're watching.

I know you work long hours at our school but I want to tell you that it is worth it as you have made our school a ......(40)...... place. I hope you stay for many more years.

Sincerely,
Malti

32. (a) thanks (b) appreciation
(c) praise (d) appeal

33. (a) wonderful (b) possible
(c) important (d) kind

34. (a) important (b) vital
(c) significant (d) outstanding

35. (a) little (b) short
(c) less (d) few

36. (a) pleasant (b) laughing
(c) smiling (d) cheering

37. (a) these (b) they
(c) this (d) those

38. (a) unhappy (b) surprised
(c) shocked (d) happy

39. (a) hard (b) harder
(c) better (d) good

40. (a) fine (b) worth
(c) finer (d) finest

Directions (Q. Nos. 41-50) Read the description of a place given below and fill suitable adjective in the gaps from the given options.

Do you have a ......(41)...... place to go, a place with family, good weather and ......(42)...... things to do like crabbing? I'm glad I do. New Jersey is my favourite place for ......(43)...... reasons.

The first reason is my family. Over half of my family lives in New Jersey. When I visit, my cousins, I laugh and play all day and night. My uncles and aunts take me to the broadwalk where we ride tall and ......(44)...... roller coasters.

We devour juicy caramel ......(45)...... apples and ......(46)...... hot dogs. My family is fun to be with.

The second reason for New Jersey being my favourite place is the weather. Instead of being hot and sweaty, it is always ......(47)...... and moist. When I think about my visits, I can just feel the crisp fall breeze in my hair. I can just see the ......(48)...... fluffy winter snow. I can just hear the soft spring trickles of rain splashing on the sidewalks. I can just feel the ......(49)...... summer sun on my face. The weather is ......(50)...... .

41. (a) pet (b) most-liked
(c) favourite (d) adored

42. (a) funny (b) interesting
(c) touring (d) pleasure

43. (a) much (b) many
(c) enough (d) more

44. (a) taller (b) longer
(c) long (d) short

45. (a) covered (b) more
(c) full (d) less

46. (a) feet long (b) foot long
(c) spicy (d) delicious

47. (a) cold (b) humid
(c) cool (d) hot

48. (a) yellow (b) shining
(c) white (d) off-white

49. (a) warm (b) hot
(c) cold (d) heat

50. (a) stet (b) amazing
(c) great (d) bad

Verbs

A verb is a word or group of words that tells about the action or the state of any noun or subject.

e.g. He ran to the store. Here, the verb 'ran' describes the action of the subject 'he'.

Verbs show what the subject is doing or what is the condition of the subject.

e.g. She is beautiful. (State)
The cat killed the mouse. (Action)
The tyre burst in the workshop. (Event)

We use verbs to say what people and things do. Verbs are 'doing' words.

Types of Verb

Verb may be broadly classified into following types:

1. **Main Verb** (Regular Verb) The verb form that indicates the nature of an action is the main verb. i.e. sell, go, read, agree etc.
   e.g. She cut an apple.
2. **Helping Verb** (Auxiliary Verb) These verbs are used along with main verbs to form meaningful sentences.
   We can explain helping verbs with the help of the table given below.

Subject	**Helping Verb in the Past Tense**	**Helping Verb in the Present Tense**	**Helping Verb in the Future Tense**
I	was	am	shall be
You	were	are	will be
He/She/It	was	is	will be
We	were	are	will be
You	were	are	will be
They	were	are	will be

3. Modals These are a type of helping verbs that are used to express ability, possibility, permission, obligation, suggestion, request etc. They give additional information about the function of the main verb. They can express different meanings in different context.

The table given below contains functions and examples of modals.

S.No.	Function	Example	Usage
1.	Necessity/Lack of necessity	need/need not	Need I say more? I need not buy any tomatoes.
2.	Advice/Suggestion	should/ought to/would/shall	You should exercise every day. You should/ought to see a doctor. If I were you, I would return the book.
3.	Prohibition/Obligation	must not/must	You must not smoke in the hospital. We must stop when the traffic light turns red.
4.	Ability	can/could	I can swim. When I was younger I could stay up all night and not get tired.
5.	Permission	may/can/could	May I take leave tomorrow? Can I use your phone please? Excuse me, could I just say something?
6.	Request	can/could/will	Can you guide me to the railway station? Could you help me to lift this heavy box? Will you please solve this problem for me?
7.	Possibility/Probability	might/could/may	I might visit America next year. Smoking could cause cancer! It may rain tomorrow! / It could rain tomorrow!
8.	Logical Assumption	must/can't	He must be very tired after such enormous work. He can't drive a car. He's not yet 18.
9.	Offer	shall	Shall I do the shopping for you?

4. Phrasal Verb A phrasal verb is a verb + preposition or adverb, which creates a different meaning from the original verb alone.

e.g. I need to get a new battery for my phone. (Verb)

Why don't we all get together for dinner tomorrow? (Phrasal Verb)

Let's Practice

Directions (Q. Nos. 1-5) Fill in the blanks with the most suitable option.

1. The girl in the white dress .... my sister.
(a) am (b) is (c) are (d) were

2. They regularly .... cricket in the evening.
(a) played (b) play (c) playing (d) will play

3. The musicians .... brilliant in their performance.
(a) was (b) is (c) were (d) did

4. She .... the seminar tomorrow.
(a) was attending (b) attended
(c) will attend (d) attends

5. I have decided to .... with my work after a short nap.
(a) carry out (b) carry over
(c) carry on (d) carry away

Directions (Q. Nos. 6-10) Choose the correct verb form of the underlined word.

6. Disha <u>choose</u> a black dress for herself.
(a) chose (b) choosed
(c) chosen (d) choosing

7. Our teacher <u>hitted</u> by a car yesterday.
(a) hit (b) hitting
(c) hitten (d) None of these

8. Roshni <u>builded</u> a new house for her doll.
(a) build (b) has build
(c) building (d) built

9. The rally was <u>lead</u> by a senior politician.
(a) led (b) leaded
(c) leading (d) None of these

10. Mother <u>hide</u> all toys in the store room.
(a) hidden (b) hided (c) hid
(d) hiding

Directions (Q. Nos. 11-15) Choose the sentence(s) with correct use of modals.

11. (i) After hours of hard work, Abhinav can get some rest.
(ii) After hours of hard work, Abhinav may get some rest.
(iii) After hours of hard work, Abhinav could get some rest.
(iv) After hours of hard work. Abhinav must get some rest.

Codes
(a) (i) (b) (ii) and (iv)
(c) (i) and (iii) (d) (iv)

12. (i) She could started learning English years ago.
(ii) She could have started learning English years ago.
(iii) She should started learning English years ago.
(iv) She should have started learning English years ago.

Codes
(a) (i) and (ii) (b) (ii) and (iii)
(c) (iii) (d) (iv)

13. (i) See carefully ! There can be duplicate keys in Dad's drawer.
(ii) See carefully ! There could be duplicate keys in Dad's drawer.
(iii) See carefully ! There would be duplicate keys in Dad's drawer.
(iv) See carefully ! There must be duplicate keys in Dad's drawer.

Codes
(a) (ii) (b) (i) and (iii)
(c) (ii) and (iii) (d) (iv)

14. (i) We can read this book.
(ii) We must read this book.
(iii) We should read this book.
(iv) We cannot read this book.

Codes
(a) (i) and (iv) (b) (ii) and (iii)
(c) (iii) and (iv) (d) All of these

15. (i) Rajat cannot play in the tournament.
(ii) Rajat has not play in the tournament.
(iii) Rajat should not play in the tournament.
(iv) Rajat was not play in the tournament.

Codes
(a) (ii) and (iii) (b) (i) and (iii)
(c) (ii) and (iv) (d) (iii) and (iv)

Directions (Q. Nos. 16-20) Given below are sentences divided into four underlined parts marked (a), (b), (c) and (d). Choose the part which contains verb.

16. I (a) am (b) twenty five (c) years old (d).

17. Her brother's (a) name (b) is (c) Paul (d).

18. There (a) are (b) twelve students (c) in my class (d).

19. It (a) is (b) a cool (c) day today (d).

20. I (a) have (b) two apples (c) in my bag (d).

Directions (Q. Nos. 21-25) Find the odd one out.

21. (a) Am (b) Are (c) Is (d) As

22. (a) Sleep (b) Talk (c) Eat (d) Can

23. (a) Will (b) Would (c) Should (d) Read

24. (a) Think (b) Could (c) Run (d) Fight

25. (a) May (b) Might (c) Drink (d) Should

26. Match the sentences in List I with their correct form of verb in List II.

	List I		List II
A.	My brother very often .... me when I am on the phone.	1.	carried
B.	We .... a kettle on the camping trip to boil soup or water.	2.	like
C.	I must .... everyday to score good marks.	3.	disturbs
D.	Young children .... to spend more time with their friends.	4.	study

Codes

	A	B	C	D		A	B	C	D
(a)	3	2	1	4	(b)	2	1	4	3
(c)	3	1	4	2	(d)	1	4	3	2

27. Complete the sentences by matching their two parts in List I and List II.

	List I		List II
A.	Each of the team members	1.	my father asked me.
B.	We could n't afford to keep our car,	2.	but nobody laughed at it.
C.	"How did you learn to drive"?	3.	received cash prizes.
D.	It was a funny situation	4.	so we sold it.

Codes

	A	B	C	D		A	B	C	D
(a)	2	1	4	3	(b)	3	4	1	2
(c)	1	4	2	3	(d)	2	1	3	4

Directions (Q. Nos. 28-31) Complete the dialogue by using the correct form of verb in the gap.

28. **Anne** Was the film good?

Julie No, I .... bored of it in the middle of the film.

(a) were getting (b) got
(c) gets (d) has got

29. **Anne** Were you pleased with the new notice?

Julie No, it .... me very unhappy.

(a) has make (b) make
(c) made (d) will making

30. **Anne** Are you hungry at the moment?

Julie No, I .... a heavy meal a couple of hours ago.

(a) have (b) has
(c) had (d) having

31. **Anne** Could you do this for me?

Julie Yes, but I can't .... the job until tomorrow.

(a) do (b) did
(c) done (d) had done

Directions (Q. Nos. 32-36) Complete the sentences with the correct phrasal verb.

32. She .... the directory for the phone number.

(a) looked into (b) looked away
(c) looked up (d) look away

33. I never .... the story about ghosts.
(a) made up (b) make for
(c) make a way (d) made into

34. Mary has .... a new dress along with matching hat.
(a) put off (b) put before
(c) put on (d) put away

35. Please .... your essay by Wednesday afternoon.
(a) hand in (b) hand over
(c) hand on (d) hand out

36. I can't quite .... the signature of my maths teacher.
(a) make up (b) make out
(c) make into (d) make over

Directions (Q. Nos. 37-40) Replace the expression underlined in each sentence by choosing the correct phrasal verb.

37. The gang of robbers escaped taking 5 million pounds.
The gang .... with 5 million pounds .
(a) get away (b) sorted out
(c) got away (d) put up

38. Manjari says she is going to visit us on Thursday.
Manjari says that she is going to .... on Thursday.
(a) hang on (b) get away
(c) sort out (d) drop in

39. Which group of words has main verbs?
(a) Sing, talk, play, would
(b) Sing, should, talk play
(c) Sing, talk, go, play
(d) Sing, talk, will, play

40. Helping verbs generally come .... the main verb.
(a) behind (b) follows
(c) before (d) in between

Directions (Q. Nos. 41-51) Read the passage given below. There are some blanks. Fill them by selecting the correct verb from the given options.

Trees ......(41)...... tall plants with hard and thick trunks. The main trunk of large trees like the mango and the banyan ......(42)...... many branches, which further ...(43)... into smaller branches. Leaves ......(44)...... on these branches. Branching ......(45)...... the tree to spread out wide on all sides.

Trees are nature's wonders and a great gift to mankind as well as to all those who depend on them. While some dependents ......(46)...... on the trees others come to them to rest or to ......(47)...... their young ones. Still others use them to raise their offsprings. Humans have ......(48)...... almost every tree for their benefit. They are ......(49)...... trees to create new factories, new townships, wider roads and railways, entertainment centres and so on. They ......(50)...... not realise that they are ......(51)...... a big mistake.

41. (a) is (b) are
(c) were (d) was

42. (a) bear (b) bears
(c) is bearing (d) are bearing

43. (a) divides (b) divided
(c) are divided (d) divide

44. (a) grows (b) grow
(c) are growing (d) grown

45. (a) caused (b) cause
(c) causes (d) is causing

46. (a) staying (b) stay
(c) are staying (d) stayed

47. (a) feed (b) fed
(c) are feeding (d) feeding

48. (a) use (b) used
(c) using (d) been using

49. (a) cut (b) cuts
(c) cutting (d) have cut

50. (a) do
(b) does
(c) did
(d) have

51. (a) making
(b) made
(c) make
(d) have made

Tenses

Tenses of a verb show the time of an event or action in a sentence. There are three main tenses: Present, Past and Future. These three main tenses can be further divided into four forms each: Simple, Continuous, Perfect and Perfect Continuous tense.

These tenses can be better explained with the help of examples as given in the following table :

Simple Present	Simple Past	Simple Future
• I play cricket. • Cats like milk. • Delhi is the capital of India. • The party starts at 9 O'clock.	• I wrote a letter to my friend. • He washed all his clothes yesterday. • We lived in Chennai for two years.	• We will go to zoo tomorrow. • She will not sing in today's function. • I will be careful.
Present Continuous	**Past Continuous**	**Future Continuous**
• You are dancing. • They are going to the market. • I am not going to the party tonight.	• Gunjan was sleeping when the doorbell rang. • Rishi was playing while his brother was watching TV. • Were you studying when I called?	• We will be waiting for you at platform when the train arrives. • Kids will be watching TV when mother cooks food in the evening.
Present Perfect	**Past Perfect**	**Future Perfect**
• I have not seen him for a long time. • No one has finished their homework. • English has become popular.	• Ronnie had looked the door before he went to the market. • She has completed her homework before she watched TV. • Mother had removed old curtains before the guests visited.	• Mother will have cooked food by the time father comes back from office. • Kids will have arranged their room by the time parents come back. • By next month, I will have received my promotion.

Present Perfect Continuous	Past Perfect Continuous	Future Perfect Continuous
• I have been waiting for the bus for last one hour. • He has been playing cricket for 5 years. • What have you been doing?	• You had been playing for over two hours before Dad arrived. • You had been waiting for pizza for one hour when I arrived.	• We will have been waiting for hours at airport before his plane arrives. • He will have been teaching in India for 15 years by the time he leaves for Australia.

Let's Practice

Directions (Q. Nos. 1-5) In the following sentences, fill in the blanks by choosing correct option.

1. Look! Sara is .... to see a movie.
(a) go (b) went
(c) going (d) will be going

2. In her right hand, Sara .... her hand bag.
(a) is carrying (b) carried
(c) carries (d) All of these

3. The handbag .... really beautiful.
(a) is (b) was
(c) Both (a) and (b) (d) None of these

4. Sara usually .... on black shoes but today she .... white trainers.
(a) put, wears (b) puts, is wearing
(c) put, was wearing (d) put, were

5. Look! She is .... an umbrella as it is.......... .
(a) takes, raining (b) taking, raining
(c) look, raining (d) none of these

Directions (Q. Nos. 6-9) Fill in the blanks with correct tense.

6. We .... to London because our friend .... us.
(a) go, has (b) went, had invited
(c) going, has been invited (d) went, has invited

7. Jane .... already typed three pages when her computer ....
(a) have, crashed (b) has, crashing
(c) had, crashed (d) is, crashing

8. I think I lost my camera when I .... down from the taxi.
(a) got (b) gotten
(c) was running (d) was getting

9. When he woke up, his mother .... already .... breakfast.
(a) has, prepares (b) is, preparing
(c) had, prepared (d) have, prepared

Directions (Q. Nos. 10-15) Replace the underlined word to make grammatically correct sentence.

10. She finally <u>finish</u> her holiday homework before the school reopened.
(a) finish (b) finished
(c) will finish (d) finishing

11. My brother <u>work</u> in a Multi-National Company (MNC).
(a) will working (b) will worked
(c) works (d) has working

12. I will be <u>visited</u> the water park along with friends on Saturday.
(a) visiting (b) will visit
(c) visits (d) visit

13. I <u>will attending</u> a marriage function in Delhi. this weekend.
(a) attending (b) will attend
(c) attend (d) has attended

14. Last weekend we <u>celebrate</u> my brother's birthday.
(a) celebrated (b) celebrates
(c) celebrating (d) will celebrate

15. Tomorrow after school I <u>go</u> to watch a football match.
(a) am going
(b) is going
(c) will going
(d) be going

Directions (Q. Nos. 16-20) Which is the correct tense for the following sentences?

16. My boss left for London yesterday.
(a) Simple present (b) Present continuous
(c) Simple past (d) None of these

17. The boys are playing Hockey.
(a) Simple past (b) Simple present
(c) Present continuous (d) Past perfect

18. We have bought a new home in South Delhi.
(a) Present continuous (b) Present perfect
(c) Future simple (d) Simple present

19. I ate lots of ice-cream at my friend's house.
(a) Present continuous (b) Simple present
(c) Present perfect (d) Simple past

20. My elder sister Nikita will celebrate her thirteenth birthday next Sunday.
(a) Simple present (b) Present perfect
(c) Simple future (d) Simple past

Directions (Q. Nos. 21-24) In each question, select the option with the correct use of tenses.

21. (a) I visit my grandmother every weekend.
(b) I visiting my grandmother every weekend.
(c) I has visited my grandmother every weekend.
(d) I will be visit my grandmother every weekend.

22. (a) He is plant a sapling in the garden.
(b) He planting a sapling in the garden.
(c) He planted a sapling in the garden.
(d) He have planted a sapling in the garden.

23. (a) He and his friends eat food in a restaurant everyday.
(b) He and his friends are eaten food in a restaurant everyday.
(c) He and his friends have eating food in a restaurant everyday.
(d) He and his friends eaten food in a restaurant everyday.

24. (a) If it sunny tomorrow we may going to the water park.
(b) If it is sunny tomorrow we may went to the water park.
(c) If it is sunny tomorrow we may go to the water park.
(d) If it is sunny tomorrow we may gone to the water park.

Directions (Q. Nos. 25-26) Read the statements and choose the correct option.

25. **Statement A** We use simple present tense to show a habit or universal truth.
Statement B We use simple past tense to show our daily habit and actions.

Codes
(a) Both A and B are true (b) Only A is true
(c) Only B is true (d) None of these

26. **Statement A** To show action going on in the past, we use present continuous tense.
Statement B For completed actions, we use present perfect tense.

Codes
(a) Both B and A are correct
(b) Both A and B are false
(c) Only B is correct
(d) None of the above

Directions (Q. Nos. 27-28) Match the sentences with their correct forms of tenses.

27.

	List I		List II
A.	I need a pair of new boots.	1.	Simple past
B.	He had repeated the test and got a better score.	2.	Present continuous
C.	Did your mother work in a restaurant?	3.	Simple present
D.	I am presently enjoying my summer holidays.	4.	Past perfect

Codes

	A	B	C	D		A	B	C	D
(a)	2	3	1	4	(b)	3	1	2	4
(c)	3	4	1	2	(d)	2	4	1	3

28.

	List I		List II
A.	She will join a new company next month.	1.	Present perfect
B.	I will be cooking food for 10 people tomorrow.	2.	Present perfect continuous
C.	They have not received any payment for the work.	3.	Future continuous
D.	He has not been washing his clothes.	4.	Simple future

Codes

	A	B	C	D		A	B	C	D
(a)	4	3	1	2	(b)	3	2	4	1
(c)	2	1	3	4	(d)	1	3	2	4

Directions (Q. Nos. 29-34) Identify tense of the underlined word from the given options.

"It's still raining ...(29)... heavily", said ...(30)... Amrita. "Presumably they will have ...(31)... to cancel the fate". "It's too late ...(32)... to cancel it", said Joshina. "They will have gathered ...(33)... all the things to sell on the stalls and must have made ...(34)... all the food."

29. (a) Simple present (b) Simple future (c) Present continuous (d) Past perfect

30. (a) Past perfect (b) Perfect continuous (c) Simple past (d) Simple future

31. (a) Future perfect (b) Simple present (c) Present perfect (d) Past perfect

32. (a) Present continuous (b) Simple present (c) Past continuous (d) Simple future

33. (a) Future continuous (b) Future perfect (c) Future perfect continuous (d) Simple past

34. (a) Simple past (b) Present perfect (c) Perfect continuous (d) Future perfect

Directions (Q. Nos. 35-50) In the paragraph given below, fill in the blanks with the correct form of the verb tense by selecting the correct option.

The British explorer James Cook was ......(35)...... in the village of Marton, Yorkshire, on 27th October 1728. But his family soon ......(36)...... to another village called Great Ayton, where Cook ......(37)...... most of his childhood.

As a teenager James Cook ......(38)...... a fascination for the sea and travelled to Whitby where he ......(39)...... employment on a coal ship.

While he was ......(40)...... in the Royal Navy, Cook ......(41)...... the command of a ship.

After the war ......(42)......, James Cook ......(43)....... the command of the ship Grenville and ......(44)...... to Newfoundland where he ......(45)...... a solar eclipse off the North American coast.

Cook ......(46)...... the details to the Royal society, England's leading scientific organisation, and won their attention.

After James Cook ......(47)...... his observations of the solar eclipse, the Royal society ......(48)...... him to lead a scientific expedition to Tahiti and ......(49)...... him in command of the HMS Endeavour.

From Tahiti James Cook then ...(50)... to explore the South Pacific.

35. (a) birth (b) born (c) borned (d) burn

36. (a) moves (b) moving (c) moved (d) has moved

37. (a) spent (b) spend (c) was spending (d) will spent

38. (a) had developed (b) develops (c) developing (d) develop

39. (a) find (b) finding (c) found (d) has found

40. (a) serving (b) serve (c) served (d) has been serving

41. (a) have (b) had (c) has (d) had commanded

42. (a) ended (b) end (c) ends (d) is ending

43. (a) has taken (b) takes (c) took (d) taken

44. (a) sailing (b) sailed (c) sails (d) sailer

45. (a) observes (b) observe (c) observed (d) observing

46. (a) sent (b) send (c) had send (d) sending

47. (a) publishes (b) had published (c) publishing (d) publish

48. (a) asks (b) asked (c) had asked (d) asking

49. (a) put (b) puts (c) putted (d) had put

50. (a) go (b) went (c) gone (d) have gone

Prepositions

Prepositions are words that show the relationship between a noun or a pronoun and some other words in a sentence. Prepositions are generally placed before a noun or a pronoun.

Some frequently used prepositions are *at, by, for, from, in, of, off, out, through, till, to, up, with* etc.

e.g. Prateek is sitting on the chair.
In the sentence, 'on' is used as a preposition as it is giving the position of Prateek in relation to the chair.

Kinds of Preposition

Prepositions may be broadly classified into following groups:

1. **Preposition of Time**
   e.g. The train will leave in a few minutes.
   I get up at 5 O'clock in the morning.
   It has been raining since morning.
   e.g. for, ago, before, until, next, last etc.
2. **Preposition of Place**
   e.g. I will wait for you at the bus stop.
   Is there anything new on the notice board?
   My parents live in Mumbai.
   e.g. by, beside, between, among, behind etc.
3. **Preposition of Movement**
   e.g. The cat suddenly jumped out the table.
   We are going to the cinema.
   All boys swimmed across the lake.
   e.g. by, through, along, into, off etc.
4. **Preposition of Other Relationship**
   e.g. You may e-mail us at info@example.com.
   At 19, he become captain of the team.
   This book is written by Chetan Bhagat.
   e.g. of, with, without, (good) at, (bad) at, through etc.

Let's Practice

Directions (Q. Nos. 1-3) In the following questions, find the appropriate preposition to complete the sentences.

1. .... the bungalow, there was an old oak tree where numerous birds had built their nests.
(a) Under (b) On
(c) Inside (d) Below

2. He was standing on the platform .... the level of the audience.
(a) under (b) below
(c) above (d) between

3. There was a name plate .... the door of the house bearing the name of the owner.
(a) at (b) on (c) of (d) along

Directions (Q. Nos. 4-6) In the following questions, fill in the blank with a suitable preposition of time.

4. She had to work hard .... her life.
(a) through (b) for
(c) throughout (d) across

5. The superfast express arrived at the station .... time.
(a) at (b) in (c) of (d) for

6. John was nowhere to be seen .... the time of Christmas.
(a) from (b) at (c) in (d) for

Directions (Q. Nos. 7-12) Fill in the blank with a suitable preposition used after a noun, verb or adjectives.

7. This restaurant is always in short supply .... food.
(a) at (b) of
(c) off (d) with

8. I will return home .... four days.
(a) before (b) after
(c) on (d) around

9. The troops opened the door .... courage.
(a) for (b) with
(c) in (d) over

10. Ronny always pays attention .... what his teacher is saying.
(a) to (b) at
(c) over (d) about

11. Walter is not mean, he is just very careful .... money.
(a) on (b) at
(c) with (d) for

12. Like many other children, my daughter is mad .... chocolate.
(a) under (b) of
(c) with (d) over

Directions (Q. Nos. 13-20) Fill in the blanks with appropriate prepositions.

13. We all laughed .... the jokes told by Mahi.
(a) in (b) with
(c) on (d) at

14. Rajeev is suffering .... malaria for last ten days.
(a) with (b) from
(c) by (d) over

15. Good English cartoons and movies leave a good impression .... young children.
(a) with (b) upon (c) at (d) after

16. Some people are very keen .... working in a team, while others are not.
(a) on (b) to (c) about (d) at

17. People who are good .... making friends usually work in the field of trade or sales.
(a) in (b) to (c) at (d) for

18. My son is mad .... science and technology; I guess he'll become an engineer.
(a) our (b) about (c) of (d) with

19. Most children are fond .... playing instead of eating during lunch break.
(a) in (b) from (c) of (d) at

20. Small children get addicted .... mobile or video games very easily.
(a) at (b) to (c) in (d) with

Directionss (Q. Nos. 21-25) Choose the sentence(s) with correct use of preposition.

21. (i) Our house is beside the railway station.
(ii) Our house is next the railway station.
(iii) Our house is across the railway station.
(iv) Our house is next to the railway station.

Codes
(a) (i) and (ii) (b) (ii) and (iii)
(c) (i) and (iii) (d) (i) and (iv)

22. (i) There is a hill behind my village.
(ii) There is a hill between my village.
(iii) There is a hill up my village.
(iv) There is a hill onto my village.

Codes
(a) (i) (b) (ii)
(c) (ii) and (iii) (d) (iii) and (iv)

23. (i) Maria goes to church on Saturdays.
(ii) Maria goes to church next Saturdays.
(iii) Maria goes to church at Saturdays.
(iv) Maria goes to church in Saturdays.

Codes
(a) (i) (b) (ii) (c) (iii) (d) (iv)

24. (i) This area becomes deserted in night.
(ii) This area becomes deserted into night.
(iii) This area becomes deserted at night.
(iv) This area becomes deserted up night.

Codes
(a) (i) (b) (ii) (c) (iii) (d) (iv)

25. (i) Mother chopped onions from a knife.
(ii) Mother chopped onions by a knife.
(iii) Mother chopped onions off a knife.
(iv) Mother chopped onions with a knife.

Codes
(a) (i) (b) (ii) (c) (iii) (d) (iv)

26. Match List I with List II to complete the sentences correctly.

	List I		List II
A.	I am not speaking	1.	you should cross it out.
B.	As this word is not needed here,	2.	I'd better take them off.
C.	Everyone complained	3.	to my neighbours.
D.	My shoes are dirty;	4.	about the unhygienic food.

Codes

	A	B	C	D		A	B	C	D
(a)	2	3	4	1	(b)	3	1	4	2
(c)	2	4	1	3	(d)	3	1	2	4

27. Fill in the blank of List I from a suitable preposition from List II to complete the sentences correctly.

	List I		List II
A.	Pay attention .... what the teacher says.	1.	on
B.	He is the man I was looking	2.	upon
C.	The cat jumped .... the chair.	3.	to
D.	The workers went .... strike to protest against the manager.	4.	for

Codes

	A	B	C	D		A	B	C	D
(a)	2	4	3	1	(b)	4	2	1	3
(c)	3	4	2	1	(d)	2	3	4	1

28. Match the words in List I with prepositions in List II as used in normal expressions.

	List I		List II
A.	endowed	1.	from
B.	superior	2.	of
C.	differ	3.	with
D.	boast	4.	to

Codes

	A	B	C	D		A	B	C	D
(a)	3	4	1	2	(b)	4	3	1	2
(c)	2	1	4	3	(d)	1	2	4	3

Directions (Q. Nos. 29-37) Complete the conversation by filling the blanks with appropriate preposition.

Dicky Did you hear ...(29)... my experience at the Neo Burger Cafe?

Angel No, and I have never heard ...(30)... the Neo Burger Cafe.

Dicky Oh, it's near the station. I was just talking ...(31)... Minni ...(32)... it. They took at least twenty minutes to bring me a burger. I don't call it quick service. I complained ...(33)... the waitress and she poured a can of cola ...(34)... me.

Angel Really? She must have had a bad day.

Dicky The manager was not there, so I've written ...(35)... him complaining ...(36)... the service. It was terrible.

Angel I wouldn't dream ...(37)... going there. I hate those burger places.

29. (a) on (b) about (c) at (d) to

30. (a) about (b) of (c) to (d) in

31. (a) with (b) to (c) about (d) in

32. (a) for (b) over (c) about (d) to

33. (a) about (b) to (c) for (d) on

34. (a) to (b) at (c) over (d) around

35. (a) to (b) with (c) at (d) about

36. (a) for (b) about (c) at (d) of

37. (a) at (b) in (c) of (d) to

Directions (Q. Nos. 38-50) Read the story and fill in the blanks with suitable preposition.

Ann was driving her truck ...(38)... the road to John's house. She was enjoying the trip, looking ...(39)... of the window at the view.

Sue was sitting ...(40)... her, holding a big cup of water. Suddenly, they hit a big bump in the road. The cup flew ...(41)... of Sue's hands. The water spilled out everywhere. It was ...(42)... top of the seat ...(43)... the two women. It was all ...(44)... the clothes they were wearing. It was even ...(45)... Sue's shoes. Her socks were wet ...(46)... her shoes. Ann stopped the truck ...(47)... the road. 'I am so sorry' said Ann. 'It looks like the water has even gone ...(48)... the seat. I didn't see that bump until it was too late. I couldn't go ...(49)... it. I had to go ...(50)... it.' 'It's alright', replied Sue. 'I should not have had water inside the truck. It's my fault'.

38. (a) in (b) with (c) down (d) around

39. (a) out (b) at (c) over (d) across

40. (a) behind (b) beside (c) between (d) among

41. (a) on (b) beside (c) out (d) over

42. (a) at (b) on (c) in (d) of

43. (a) between (b) under (c) among (d) in

44. (a) above (b) over (c) inside (d) at

45. (a) in (b) at (c) of (d) out

46. (a) outside (b) in (c) inside (d) at

47. (a) near (b) beside (c) between (d) at

48. (a) down behind (b) all over (c) outside (d) beside

49. (a) above (b) around (c) over (d) at

50. (a) over (b) above (c) about (d) to

Conjunctions

Conjunctions are joining words in a sentence. They are used to join two or more sentences, words or phrases. They are also known as 'connectors'.

Conjunctions help in making sentences shorter and better directed.

e.g.

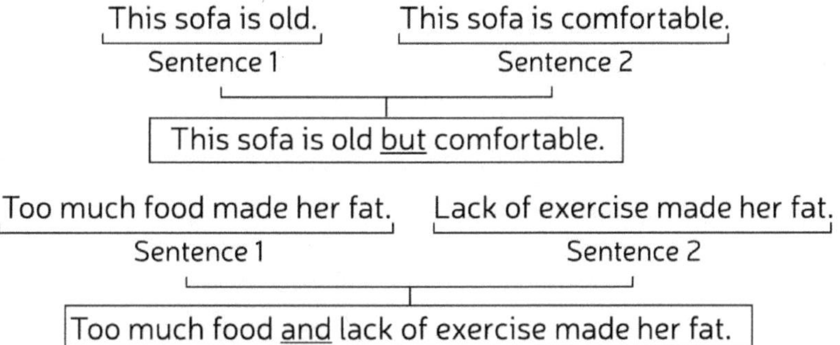

Conjunctions are of following types :

1. **Coordinating Conjunctions**

   These conjunctions are used to join sentence elements that are grammatically equal. Coordinating conjunctions join words to words, phrases to phrases and clauses to clauses.

   e.g. Mona likes to eat pizza. (Sentence 1) Mona likes to eat burger. (Sentence 2)

   Mona likes to eat pizza <u>and</u> burger.

   Coordinating conjunctions are only seven and can easily be memorised by remembering 'FAN BOYS'.

   F – For A – And N – Nor B – But

   O – Or Y – Yet S – So

2. **Correlative Conjunctions**

These conjunctions are used in pair and require equal or parallel structure after each one.

e.g. Kavya didn't come to the party. Mohit didn't come to the party.

Sentence 1 Sentence 2

Neither Kavya nor peter came to the party.

e.g. either-or, both-and, not only-but also etc.

3. **Subordinating Conjunctions**

Subordinating conjunctions are used to join two clauses. They make one clause dependent or subordinate upon the other.

e.g. Mihir is not well. He didn't go to the school.

Clause 1 Clause 2

Because Mihir is not well, he didn't go to the school.

e.g. after, although, unless, until, so that etc.

Let's Practice

Directions (Q. Nos. 1-16) Fill in the blanks by choosing correct option.

1. .... I shall drive .... I shall take a train.

(a) Not only ...... but also (b) Not ..... but
(c) Whether ..... or (d) Either .... or

2. .... my car .... bike need to be repaired.

(a) Either .... or (b) Both .... and
(c) Not .... but (d) Whether .... or

3. Come early tomorrow .... we can practise for annual day.

(a) and (b) until
(c) although (d) so that

4. We worked continuously .... the teacher asked us to stop.

(a) unless (b) although
(c) until (d) while

5. He may be talented .... he is very arrogant.

(a) and (b) so that (c) yet (d) but

6. .... we were very hungry, we did not demand food.

(a) Until (b) Yet (c) Although (d) As

7. He did not join us for the movie .... he had already seen it.

(a) once (b) though
(c) although (d) because

8. He will show us around himself .... send someone else.

(a) and (b) if (c) or (d) so

9. She could not find the book she wanted .... she borrowed a magazine instead.

(a) so (b) and (c) but (d) so that

10. .... the teacher explained the lesson several times, some of the students still did not understand it.

(a) Although (b) Even if
(c) Unless (d) Since

11. I don't think Sam will remember about the project .... you remind him.

(a) so (b) if (c) unless (d) lest

12. Our family had finished dinner, ... we watched TV.

(a) unless (b) until (c) so (d) yet

13. Brijesh confidently replied to all the questions, ... he was an expert.
(a) although (b) as though
(c) unless (d) but

14. Ravi waited .... Kamal woke up.
(a) while (b) until
(c) yet (d) unless

15. .... Tinku is very good at Science, Ranjit is good at Mathematics.
(a) Until (b) Although
(c) While (d) Since

16. We stayed at home .... it was raining heavily.
(a) therefore (b) though
(c) yet (d) because

Directions (Q. Nos. 17-22) Choose the option which should replace the underlined word to make sentence correct.

17. They worked hard for the test as though they failed.
(a) unless (b) however
(c) while (d) yet

18. She goes to the tennis club because she likes to play tennis.
(a) though (b) even though
(c) although (d) None of these

19. Please look at the map when you'll lost.
(a) it (b) otherwise
(c) unless (d) until

20. Her baby cannot fall asleep yet she stays in the room.
(a) unless (b) until (c) because (d) but

21. He reads magazines rather than he doesn't like to read book.
(a) unless (b) until (c) so (d) but

22. He is very famous even he is still nice.
(a) unless (b) until (c) although (d) yet

Directions (Q. Nos. 23-26) Find the odd one out in the following options.

23. (a) Since (b) Until
(c) While (d) To

24. (a) Neither (b) Either
(c) Some (d) Or

25. (a) Weather (b) Where (c) Whether (d) Whenever

26. (a) Boot (b) Bite (c) Bat (d) But

Directions (Q. Nos. 27-33) In the following questions, select the option with the correctly used conjunction.

27. (a) This is an expensive although useless book.
(b) This is an expensive and useless book.
(c) This is an expensive but useless book.
(d) This is an expensive while useless book.

28. (a) You will not watch the movie but you finish your home work.
(b) You will not watch the movie as you finish your home work.
(c) You will not watch the movie unless you finish your home work.
(d) You will not watch the movie if you finish your home work.

29. (a) They reached the station but the train had left.
(b) They reached the station and the train had left.
(c) They reached the station so the train had left.
(d) They reached the station or the train had left.

30. (a) Both John and Lee wants to lose as they are very competitive.
(b) Neither John nor Lee wants to lose as they are very competitive.
(c) Either John or Lee wants to lose as they are very competitive.
(d) Whether John or Lee wants to lose, as they are very competitive.

31. (a) Our principal is quite firm as she is kind also.
(b) Our principal is quite firm although she is kind also.
(c) Our principal is quite firm, but she is kind also.
(d) Our principal is quite firm and she is kind also.

32. (a) She has not spoken to us while we had the argument.
(b) She has not spoken to us for we had the argument.
(c) She has not spoken to us since we had the argument.
(d) She has not spoken to us where we had the argument.

33. (a) Father locked the garage door because no one could tamper with the car.
(b) Father locked the garage door, but no one could tamper with the car.
(c) Father locked the garage door so that no one could tamper with the car.
(d) Father locked the garage door atleast no one could tamper with the car.

Directions (Q. Nos. 34-35) Identify the correct (identified as T for 'True') and incorrect. (identified as F for 'False') sentences and choose the correct option.

34. 1. He left the field so of getting hurt.
2. He left the school because his parents could not pay his fees.
3. He saved some bread so that he should not go hungry.
4. She must weep but she will die.

(a) TFTF (b) FTTF (c) TTFF (d) FFTT

35. 1. He ran away since he had stolen the money.
2. Answer the first question before you proceed further.
3. You will pass unless you work hard.
4. For you say so I must believe it.

(a) FTFT (b) TFTF (c) TTFF (d) FFTT

Directions (Q. Nos. 36-40) A sentence has been divided into four parts. Choose the part which is not correct.

36. She left (a)/ the party in (b)/ the middle yet (c)/ she was bored. (d)

37. You will (a)/ do well (b)/ and you (c)/ study hard. (d)

38. Surbhi was (a)/ crying unless (b)/ she had (c)/ lost her purse. (d)

39. The spectators (a)/ went home (b)/ whenever the match (c)/ was over. (d)

40. Gunjan waited (a)/ after his (b)/ father woke (c)/ up. (d)

Directions (Q. Nos. 41-42) Match List I with List II and choose the correct option.

41.

List I	List II
A. He is rich .... honest.	1. if
B. You will not be able to score good marks .... you do not study.	2. but
C. The rainy weather is cool ..... humid.	3. although
D. The teacher scolded Ronnie ...... he had submitted his home work in time.	4. and

Codes

	A	B	C	D		A	B	C	D
(a)	2	3	1	4	(b)	4	3	1	2
(c)	4	1	2	3	(d)	2	1	4	3

42.

List I	List II
A. The Sun shone again .... the rain was over.	1. because
B. It is cold .... snow is falling.	2. all well as
C. You are naughty ..... disobedient.	3. as
D. The teacher was angry .... the students were shouting.	4. after

Codes

	A	B	C	D		A	B	C	D
(a)	3	2	4	1	(b)	4	1	2	3
(c)	4	3	2	1	(d)	3	4	1	2

Directions (Q. Nos. 43-47) Read the story given below and fill in the blanks with the correct conjunctions.

Long Long ago, there lived a poor boy called Dick Whittington. He often had nothing to eat .....(43)..... he had lost both his father and mother. One day, he heard of the great city of London .....(44)....., even the streets were paved with gold. Dick decided to go to London to seek his fortune. London was a big .....(45)..... busy city, full of people, both rich .....(46)..... poor. .....(47)..... Dick roamed in the streets, he couldn't find any gold. He fell a sleep on the steps of a great house because he was tired, cold and hungry. This house belonged to Mr. Fitzwarren, a rich merchant who was also a good and generous man. He took Dick into his house and gave him work as a servant boy.

43. (a) and (b) as well (c) since (d) although

44. (a) where (b) which (c) that (d) and

45. (a) but (b) and (c) because (d) as

46. (a) as well as (b) and (c) though (d) if

47. (a) Because (b) If (c) As (d) Unless

Punctuation

Punctuation means the right use of putting marks or symbols to clarify the meaning of a sentence.

The following are the common punctuation marks

1. Capital Letter It is used at the beginning of the sentence.
   e.g. The fruit basket contains lots of fruits.
2. Full Stop (.) It is used to mark the end of an assertive or imperative sentence.
   e.g. He was playing cricket the whole day.
3. Comma (,) It is used to indicate a break or pause in a sentence, list items in a series, separate two or more adjectives describing a noun etc.
   e.g. It was a long, dull and tiring journey.
4. Apostrophe (') It is used to indicate the omission of one or more letters in a word.
   e.g. Don't give up.
5. Question Mark (?) It is used at the end of an interrogative sentence to indicate a query.
   e.g. Have you finished your work?
6. Exclamation Mark (!) It is used at the end of an exclamatory sentence to show feelings like anger, surprise or joy.
   e.g. What a horrible summer!
7. Quotation Marks (" ") These are used to enclose a direct quotation spoken by a person.
   e.g. "I would rather die", he exclaimed, "than help any terrorist".
8. Semi colon (;) It is used to separate parts of sentence which already has commas.
   e.g. She likes apples; however she does not like bananas.

   Note Other punctuation marks are colons (:), dash(—) etc.

Let's Practice

Directions (Q. Nos. 1-10) In the questions given below, select the option which is correctly punctuated.

1. (a) She didnt hear childrens cries.
(b) She didnt hear children's cries.
(c) She didn't hear childrens cries.
(d) She didn't hear children's cries.

2. (a) The dogs bark was far worse than it's bite.
(b) The dog's bark was far worse than it's bite.
(c) The dog's bark was far worse than its bite.
(d) The dogs bark was far worse than it's bite.

3. (a) Dont you hear that I am leaving now?
(b) Don't you hear that I am leaving now!
(c) Don't you hear that I m leaving now.
(d) Don't you hear that I am leaving. Now!

4. (a) Butter which is lighter than water, floats on it's surface.
(b) Butter, which is lighter than water, floats on its surface.
(c) Butter, which is lighter than water, floats on it's surface.
(d) Butter which is lighter than water floats on it's surface.

5. (a) Can we leave the room Miss!
(b) Can we leave the Room. Miss!
(c) Can we leave the Room, Miss!
(d) Can we leave the room, Miss?

6. (a) The paper scissors and pencils belong to the top drawer!
(b) The paper scissors and pencils belong to the top drawer.
(c) The paper, scissors and pencils belong to the top drawer.
(d) The paper, scissors and pencils, belong to the top drawer?

7. (a) The team's major concerns this year, however, are staying healthy.
(b) The teams major concerns this year however are staying healthy.
(c) The team's major concerns this year however; are, staying healthy.
(d) the team's major concerns this year however, are staying healthy.

8. (a) Our class enjoyed reading the poem dreams by langston hughes.
(b) Our class enjoyed reading the poem 'dreams' by Langston Hughes.
(c) Our class enjoyed reading the poem 'Dreams' by Langston Hughes.
(d) Our class enjoyed reading the poem "dreams" by langston Hughes?

9. (a) We have really low prices this week!
(b) We have really, low prices this week.
(c) We have really low prices this week.
(d) We have really low prices this week?

10. (a) Three major cities of UP, Varanasi, Lucknow and Agra make up the crucial vote bank for BJP.
(b) Three major cities of UP-Varanasi, Lucknow and Agra- make up the crucial vote bank of BJP.
(c) Three major cities of UP, varanasi, Lucknow, Agra make up, the crucial vote bank of BJP.
(d) Three major cities of UP Varanasi, Lucknow and Agra make up the crucial, vote bank of BJP?

Directions (Q. Nos. 11-15) In the following questions, choose the appropriate punctuation mark for the sentence.

11. I think it is going to rain tomorrow
(a) Full stop
(b) Exclamation mark
(c) Question mark
(d) Comma

12. When are you going to take out the trash
(a) Exclamation mark (b) Question mark
(c) Full stop (d) Capital letter

13. Hey everybody, look at me
(a) Question mark (b) Full stop
(c) Comma (d) Exclamation mark

14. I like oranges bananas and mangoes.
(a) Full stop (b) Comma
(c) Exclamation mark (d) Question mark

15. I am so excited! our team entered the quarter finals.
(a) Full stop (b) Comma
(c) Capital letter (d) Exclamation mark

Directions (Q. Nos. 16-17) Choose the correct option to select the word that needs a capital letter in the sentence.

16. disha and neelu are very close friends.
(a) disha (b) neelu
(c) friends (d) Both 'a' and 'b'

17. sunil gavaskar's son has also joined national cricket team.
(a) son (b) sunil gavaskar's
(c) national (d) None of these

Directions (Q. Nos. 18-19) In each question, select the option with the correctly used commas.

18. (a) I have been to France-Germany-China and Spain.
(b) I have been to France-Germany-China and Spain.
(c) I have been to France, Germany, China and Spain.
(d) I have been to France-Germany, China and Spain.

19. (a) I said that she is intelligent not pretty.
(b) I said that she is, intelligent not pretty.
(c) I said that, she is intelligent not pretty.
(d) I said that she is intelligent, not pretty.

Directions (Q. Nos. 20-21) Select the options with the correct use of inverted commas in the sentences.

20. (a) Steven shouted, "I don't want" to clean my room.
(b) Steven shouted, "I don't want to clean my room."
(c) Steven shouted, I don't want to "clean my room."
(d) Steven shouted, I don't want to clean "my room."

21. (a) "There are three more cup cakes", the teacher said.
(b) There are "three more cup cakes" the teacher said.
(c) There are three more cup cakes, "the teacher" said.
(d) There are "three" more cup cakes the Teacher said.

Directions (Q. Nos. 22-23) Identify the option which has the question mark at the correct place in the following sentences.

22. (a) What? are you doing next weekend.
(b) What are you? doing next weekend.
(c) What are you doing next weekend?
(d) What are you doing? next weekend

23. (a) Are you going? to meet the principal
(b) Are? you going to meet the principal?
(c) Are you going to meet the principal.
(d) Are you going to meet the principal?

Directions (Q. Nos. 24-25) Select the option which corrects the mistake in the use of apostrophe in the given sentence.

24. Mr. John's daughter is my daughters best friend.
(a) John's (b) friend's
(c) daughter's (d) Both 'a' and 'c'

25. Dont you dare disturb me while I am in the office.
(a) I'm (b) Do'nt
(c) Don't (d) None of these

26. Choose the correct option after matching the sentences with the appropriate punctuation marks.

	List I (Sentence)		List II (Punctuation mark)
A.	When is your birthday (...)	1.	Full stop
B.	Wow (...) the ice-cream it is my favourite.	2.	Comma
C.	The cat jumped on the fence (...)	3.	Exclamation mark
D.	I bought a juicy apple (...) a mango and a ripe banana.	4.	Question Mark

Codes

	A	B	C	D		A	B	C	D
(a)	3	1	2	4	(b)	4	3	1	2
(c)	2	3	1	4	(d)	1	3	4	2

Directions (Q. Nos. 27-31) Read each sentence given below. Mark the option which shows the correct punctuation and capitalisation for the underlined word or words.

27. <u>tom's wife</u> works in the same office as my brother.
(a) Toms wife (b) Tom's wife
(c) toms wife (d) None of these

28. "<u>Don't give</u> up now", the teacher told us.
(a) don't give (b) Don't give
(c) do not give (d) None of these

29. <u>Ann'as</u> mother's shopping list is too long.
(a) Anna's (b) Annas
(c) Annas' (d) None of these

30. The boys were taken to Dean Jefferson's office to explain their, fight.

(a) their, fight (b) their fight?
(c) their fight (d) Their fight

31. "Don't even think about parking Here," the sign commanded.

(a) Here (b) here
(c) here", (d) here!

32. Which of the following options uses the apostrophe correctly?

(a) The professors dogs are barking at the shadow.
(b) The professors' dogs are barking at the shadow.
(c) The professor's dogs are barking at the shadow.
(d) The professors dog's are barking at the shadow.

33. Which of the following options uses the exclamation mark correctly?

(a) That show! was good. I can't wait to go back again.
(b) That show was good! I can't wait to go back again.
(c) That show was! good. I can't wait to go back again.
(d) That show was good I can't wait to go back again!

34. Which of the following options uses the comma correctly?

(a) The cupboard contains worn clothes, old shoes and dirty hats.
(b) The cupboard contains, worn clothes, old shoes and dirty hats.
(c) The cupboard, contains worn clothes, old shoes and dirty hats.
(d) The, cupboard contains clothes old shoes and dirty hats.

Directions (Q. Nos. 35-40) Which is not punctuated, a sentence is followed by four options which are punctuated. Select the option which is correctly punctuated.

35. we really should be going now she said

(a) We really should be going now, she said.
(b) "We really should be going now", she said.
(c) "We really should be going" now she said.
(d) We really should be goings now! she said.

36. i dont like vanilla ice cream

(a) I dont like vanilla ice cream.
(b) I don't like vanilla ice cream.
(c) I dont like vanilla ice cream!
(d) I don't like vanilla ice cream?

37. are we there yet she asked

(a) "Are we there", yet she asked.
(b) Are we there yet, she asked.
(c) "Are we there yet", she asked.
(d) "Are we there yet", she asked?

38. you should not believe everything you hear

(a) You should not believe everything you hear.
(b) You should not believe, everything you hear.
(c) You should not believe everything, you hear?
(d) You should not believe everything you hear?

39. its such a beautifully sunny day that ive decided to go for a picnic

(a) It's such a beautifully sunny day that I've decided to go for a picnic.
(b) Its such a beautifully sunny day that Ive decided to go for a picnic.
(c) Its such a beautifully sunny day that I've decided to go for a picnic!
(d) It's such a beautifully sunny day, that I've decided to go, for a picnic.

40. didnt you hear that theyre leaving tomorrow

(a) Didn't you hear that they're leaving tomorrow?
(b) "Didn't you hear that they're leaving tomorrow."
(c) Didnt you hear that theyre leaving tomorrow?
(d) Didn't you hear that theyre leaving tomorrow!

Directions (Q.Nos. 41-45) Fill the blanks with correct punctuation marks to make sentences meaningful.

What a pleasant day it was ....(41).... Shalini, Ahana .....(42)..... Rashi and Garima were playing in the ground .....(43)..... All of a sudden .....(44).... Garima asked, "Do you want to play a new game today" .....(45)... .

41. (a) Exclamation mark (b) Full stop
(c) Question mark (d) None of these

42. (a) Colon (b) Semi colon
(c) Apostrophe (d) None of these

43. (a) Comma (b) Full stop
(c) Semi colon (d) None of these

44. (a) Colon (b) Quotation mark
(c) Comma (d) Full stop

45. (a) Full stop
(b) Exclamation mark
(c) Apostrophe
(d) Question mark

Active and Passive Voice

Voice is related to the verb in a sentence. It tells us whether a subject is in action actively or passively.

Active Voice is used when the subject performs an action.

e.g. The boy throws the ball. (Active)

In Passive Voice, the object becomes the subject of the action.

e.g. The ball is thrown by the boy. (Passive)

In the first sentence, the boy is active subject. In the second sentence, the ball which was the object in the first sentence, becomes the subject.

Here is another example The workers have painted the house (Active)

The house has been painted by the workers. (Passive)

In the first sentence, the workers is active subject. In the second sentence, the house which was the object in the first sentence, becomes the subject.

Present Tense	**Simple**	**Continuous**
Active	He makes tea.	He is making tea.
Passive	Tea is made by him.	Tea is being made by him.
Past Tense		
Active	He made tea.	He was making tea.
Passive	Tea was made by him.	Tea was being made by him.
Future Tense		
Active	He will make tea.	He will be making tea.
Passive	Tea will be made by him.	(no passive)

Let's Practice

Directions (Q. Nos. 1-5) Fill in the blanks with suitable passive verb forms from the options given below.

1. English .... all over the world.
(a) is speak (b) is spoke
(c) is spoken (d) None of these

2. All the school rooms .... by the staff daily.
(a) is cleaned (b) are cleaned
(c) was cleaned (d) None of these

3. All the files .... neatly .... by my peon.
(a) is/kept (b) are/kept
(c) was/kept (d) None of these

4. Macbeth .... by Shakespeare.
(a) was written (b) wrote
(c) is written (d) were written

5. New cars .... by thieves.
(a) is stolen (b) was stolen
(c) are stolen (d) None of these

Directions (Q. Nos. 6-10) Choose the option to correctly rewrite the following newspaper reports using passive forms of the verbs underlined.

6. Lakhs of people <u>celebrated</u> International Yoga day on 21st June all over the world.
International Yoga day .... on 21st June by lakhs of people all over the world.
(a) is celebrated (b) is being celebrated
(c) was celebrated (d) celebrated

7. Thieves <u>held</u> the manager of the Claridges Hotel at gunpoint yesterday.
The manager of Claridges hotel .... at gun point yesterday by thieves.
(a) was held (b) were held
(c) is being held (d) is held

8. The thieves <u>took away</u> around 50 lakhs rupees from the hotel safe at gunpoint.
Around 50 lakhs rupees .... by the thieves from the hotel safe at gunpoint.
(a) was taken away (b) is taken away
(c) were taken away (d) None of these

9. Prime Minister Narendra Modi <u>refused</u> selfies on Yoga day.
Selfies on Yoga day .... by Prime Minister, Narendra Modi.
(a) are refused
(b) was refused
(c) is refused
(d) were refused

10. Hundreds of nurses in UK <u>face</u> deportation.
Deportation .... by hundreds of nurses in UK.
(a) was faced (b) is faced
(c) were being faced (d) None of these

Directions (Q. Nos. 11-14) Change the following sentences into passive voice by choosing appropriate option.

11. My uncle will review the case.
(a) The case is being reviewed by my uncle.
(b) My uncle reviewed the case.
(c) The case will be reviewed by my uncle.
(d) The case has been reviewed by my uncle.

12. Karina squeezed the toothpaste with all her strength.
(a) The toothpaste was squeezed with all her strength by Karina.
(b) The toothpaste has been squeezed with all her strength by Karina.
(c) The toothpaste had been squeezed with all her strength by Karina.
(d) The toothpaste will be squeezed with all her strength by Karina.

13. Jack usually dumps his dresses on the bed.
(a) The dresses are usually being dumped on the bed by Jack.
(b) The dresses have been usually dumped on the bed by Jack on the bed.
(c) The dresses are usually dumped by Jack on the bed.
(d) The dresses had been usually being dumped by Jack on the bed.

14. The students are reading comics.
(a) The comics are read by the students.
(b) The students have been reading comics.
(c) The comics will be read by the students
(d) The comics are being read by the students.

Directions (Q. Nos. 15-19) An informal letter is given below with some blanks. Complete this letter with a passive form of verb tense.

Dear Ruby,

How are you? We are having a lovely time. We are being very well looked after by our hosts. We ......(15)...... sightseeing and we ......(16)...... to some of their friends who ......(17)...... us feel very comfortable and welcome. Last night we ......(18)...... to a water park, which is one of the landmarks of this city. We had food in a famous restaurant where dishes ......(19)...... to our taste. We plan to spend three days here before moving to the next destination. I'll have lots more to tell you when we get back. Take care.

Ravi

15. (a) was taken (b) taken
(c) were taken (d) are taken

16. (a) are introduced (b) is introduced
(c) was introduced (d) were introduced

17. (a) has made (b) make
(c) have made (d) had made

18. (a) was taken (b) were taken
(c) are taken (d) taken

19. (a) were cooked (b) was cooked
(c) are cooked (d) is cooked

Directions (Q. Nos. 20-23) Read the following instructions carefully and complete the paragraph by using passive voice.

How to Wrap Gifts With a Fabric

1. Using scissors, cut the fabric into a rough circle or square of adequate size.
2. Add several inches or centimeters more for gathering of the fabric.
3. Gather the fabric around the gift.
4. Fold into place.
5. Secure the gathered fabric at the top of the gift with a ribbon or similar item.

To wrap a gift with fabric first of all the ......(20)..... into a rough circle or square of proper size. For gathering of the fabric ...... (21) ...... at the top or side of the package. After that the fabric .... (22) ...... into place. Finally, to give the packing a beautiful touch, the ...... (23) ..... with a ribbon or similar item.

20. (a) cut the fabric
(b) fabric is to be cut
(c) fabric should be cut
(d) fabric was to be cut

21. (a) several inches or centimeters are to be added
(b) several inches is to be added
(c) several inches was to be added
(d) several inches or meters were to be added

22. (a) has to be folded
(b) is to be folded
(c) folded
(d) was to be folded

23. (a) gift is to be tied
(b) tie the gift
(c) gift should be tied
(d) gift was to be tied

Directions (Q. Nos. 24-28) Change the following sentences into active voice by selecting the appropriate option.

24. By whom was the job done?
(a) Who done this job?
(b) Who does this job?
(c) Who did this job?
(d) Who will do the job?

25. Can the door be broken by you?
(a) Can you break the door?
(b) Did you break the door?
(c) You can break the door?
(d) You broke the door?

26. Is English being spoken by him?
(a) He is speaking English.
(b) Is he speaking English?
(c) He was speaking English.
(d) He speaks English.

27. A banana is eaten by her.
(a) She ate a banana.
(b) She will eat a banana.
(c) She eats a banana.
(d) She is eating a banana.

28. Your shoes need to be cleaned properly.
(a) You should clean your shoes.
(b) Your shoes need cleaning properly.
(c) Your shoes are needed by you to be cleaned properly.
(d) You need to clean your shoes properly.

29. Match List I with List II for making the correct form of voice.

List I	List II
A. Films ...... in the cinema hall.	1. are found
B. Sharks ...... in the sea.	2. is spoken
C. Lesson ...... in the class.	3. are shown
D. Italian ...... in Italy.	4. are taught

Codes

	A	B	C	D		A	B	C	D
(a)	2	1	3	4	(b)	3	1	2	4
(c)	3	1	4	2	(d)	4	1	2	3

Directions (Q. Nos. 30-40) In the passages given below complete the sentences by choosing the appropriate option.

Passage 1

There is a chimpanzee which ......(30)..... "Bubbles". It .....(31)...... by Michael Johnson. It ......(32)..... in his home. It ......(33)...... every day by Michael Johnson himself. It .....(34)...... in funny clothes. It .....(35) ...... that "Bubbles" is Michael Johnson's only friend.

30. (a) called (b) is called (c) is being called (d) was called

31. (a) is owned (b) owns (c) is being owned (d) were owned

32. (a) kept (b) is kept (c) was kept (d) were kept

33. (a) is fed (b) fed (c) has been fed (d) was fed

34. (a) was always dressed (b) were always dressed (c) are always dressed (d) is always dressed

35. (a) is being said (b) said (c) is said (d) was said

Passage 2

The Titanic was built in 1912. It ......(36)...... in a new way and it ......(37)...... to be unsinkable. Because of this, it ......(38)...... enough life-boats for the passengers and crew. The hull ......(39)...... by a collision with a huge iceberg and the ship sank very fast. A total of 1513 people ......(40)...... that day. It was one of the biggest tragedies of the decade.

36. (a) built (b) is being built (c) was build (d) had been built

37. (a) considered (b) were considered (c) has been considered (d) was considered

38. (a) was given (b) was not given (c) given (d) has been given

39. (a) was damaged (b) is being damaged (c) was being damaged (d) has been damaged

40. (a) had been drowned (b) has been drowned (c) was damaged (d) were drowned

Directions (Q. Nos. 41-42) Choose the option which correctly changes voice of the question sentence.

41. Who taught you English?

(a) By whom were you taught English?
(b) By whom has you taught English?
(c) By whom have you taught English?
(d) By whom had you taught English?

42. The host received guests in the reception area.

(a) Guests have received by the host in the reception area.
(b) Guests had received by the host in the reception area.
(c) Guests have receive by the host in the reception area.
(d) Guests were received by the host in the reception area.

Directions (Q. Nos. 43-44) Some sentences are given in both active and passive voices. Identify them and choose the correct option. [A-Active, P-Passive]

43. (i) All students answered the question.
(ii) Shakespeare wrote many plays.
(iii) The man was hit by a truck.
(iv) The thief was caught.

(a) A P A P (b) P A A P (c) A A P P (d) A A A P

44. (i) The shopkeeper sells milk and butter.
(ii) The spider was killed by a lizard.
(iii) He was not invited in the party.
(iv) A letter was written to Municipal Commissioner.

(a) A A P P (b) A P A P (c) A P P P (d) A A A P

Vocabulary

Vocabulary, in general, refers to all words used in a language.

e.g. The vocabulary of English is getting richer day by day.

A person's vocabulary refers to set of words within a language that he/she is familiar to. Vocabulary can be described as oral vocabulary or reading vocabulary.

Oral vocabulary refers to the words, we use in speaking or recognise in listening and reading. Reading vocabulary refers to the words we recognise in print.

Vocabulary portion will contain exercise in correct use of words, spellings, analogy and jumbled words.

Let's Practice

Directions (Q. Nos. 1-5) Choose the correctly spelt word from the given options.

1. (a) Vegetebles (b) Vagetebles (c) Vegitables (d) Vegetables

2. (a) Carbun (b) Carban (c) Carbon (d) Karbon

3. (a) Accidently (b) Accidentally (c) Accedently (d) Acidently

4. (a) Coliflower (b) Kauliflower (c) Cauliflower (d) Cauleflour

5. (a) Continuus (b) Continuous (c) Continus (d) Cuntinuus

Directions (Q. Nos. 6-10) Fill the blanks by choosing the correctly spelt word from the options given below.

6. The .... is very pleasant.
(a) whether (b) weather (c) weathur (d) wether

7. Thursday comes after .... in a week.
(a) Wednasday (b) Whensday (c) Whednesday (d) Wednesday

8. "Has my friend left any ...., Mom?"
(a) massage (b) mesage
(c) message (d) messege

9. He was .... after running for a mile.
(a) tried (b) tiered
(c) tired (d) tier

10. The hot dogs tasted ....
(a) awfull (b) awefull
(c) aawful (d) awful

Directions (Q. Nos. 11-13) Find out the correctly spelt word from the options given below.

11. (a) Annay (b) Bigen
(c) Brave (d) Prity

12. (a) Chief (b) Onest
(c) Caword (d) Trew

13. (a) Heap (b) Joyful
(c) Assist (d) All of these

Directions (Q. Nos. 14-15) Select the wrongly spelt word from the options given below.

14. (a) Foolish (b) Silly
(c) Panic (d) Unnite

15. (a) Mimic (b) Sqaush
(c) Immitate (d) Milk

Directions (Q. Nos. 16-20) Words that sound the same, but with different meaning are called homophones. Fill in the blanks with the correct word from the homophones given in the options.

16. By the time we went .... the store was closed.
(a) their (b) there
(c) Both (a) and (b) (d) Neither (a) nor (b)

17. I wish you .... turn down the loud music.
(a) would (b) wood
(c) wooed (d) None of these

18. The lion kept an eye on both his ....
(a) preys (b) prays
(c) praise (d) None of these

19. The monkey wanted to break off the .... to eat it.
(a) pair (b) pare
(c) pear (d) None of these

20. When are you going .... the party?
(a) two (b) too
(c) to (d) None of these

Directions (Q. Nos. 21-25) In the following questions a relationship is given between the words. You have to find option which has the same relationship as given in question.

21. Glove : Hand
(a) Neck : Collar (b) Tie : Shirt
(c) Socks : Feet (d) Coat : Pocket

22. Letter : Word
(a) Page : Book (b) Product : Factory
(c) Club : People (d) Homework : School

23. Silence : Sound
(a) Quiet : Peace (b) Darkness : Light
(c) Talk : Whisper (d) Sing : Dance

24. Train : Track
(a) Water : Boat (b) Bullet : Barrel
(c) Idea : Brain (d) Fame : Television

25. Chalk : Blackboard
(a) Type : Point (b) Table : Chair
(c) Door : Handle (d) Pen : Paper

Directions (Q. Nos. 26-30) In the following questions two objects related to each other are given. Also a third object is given with four alternatives. Find out the alternative which will be in the same relation with the third object as the relationship between first and second objects.

26. Curd : Milk : : Shoe : ?
(a) Leather (b) Cloth (c) Jute (d) Silver

27. Malaria : Mosquito : : Cholera : ?
(a) Water (b) Soil
(c) Environment (d) Smoke

28. Reading : Knowledge : : Work : ?
(a) Money (b) Employment
(c) Time (d) Engagement

29. Dress : Body : : Bangles : ?
(a) Glass (b) Lady
(c) Wrist (d) Beauty

30. Flower : Bud : : Fruit : ?
(a) Seed (b) Tree
(c) Stem (d) Root

Directions (Q. Nos. 31-35) Choose the odd one out from the following options.

31. (a) Cap (b) Turban (c) Hat (d) Watch

32. (a) Curd (b) Butter (c) Oil (d) Cream

33. (a) Platform (b) Park (c) Bus stand (d) Dock

34. (a) Tall (b) Small (c) Huge (d) Sharp

35. (a) Car (b) Ship (c) Aeroplane (d) Fuel

Directions (Q. Nos. 36-40) Pick up the one word substitution for the group of words given below.

36. People who live next door
(a) Crowd (b) Parents
(c) Neighbours (d) None of these

37. A student who runs away from school
(a) Pedestrian (b) Truant
(c) Skipper (d) Runner

38. A person who belongs to a foreign country
(a) Alien (b) Foreigner
(c) National (d) None of these

39. Piece of land planted with fruit tree
(a) Garden (b) Lawn
(c) Orchard (d) None of these

40. A piece of writing which is difficult to read
(a) Negligible (b) Illegible
(c) Ineligible (d) Incorrigible

Directions (Q. Nos. 41-45) Find out the correctly spelt word from the given options.

41. (a) pesimistic (b) seperate (c) examination (d) victrous

42. (a) comprihension (b) conjunction (c) difident (d) crampled

43. (a) cummander (b) silki (c) highlight (d) pruvoke

44. (a) cunclusion (b) graitness (c) malaria (d) edminister

45. (a) concened (b) pauper (c) acomodate (d) cumplaint

Directions (Q. Nos. 46-50) Choose the correct option.

46. As 'bravery' is related to 'courage', similarly 'afraid' is related to
(a) trust (b) traitor
(c) coward (d) fearful

47. As 'moon' is related to 'satellite', similarly 'earth' is related to
(a) planet (b) sun
(c) mars (d) solar system

48. As 'elbow' is related to 'arm', similarly 'knee' is related to
(a) walking (b) finger
(c) leg (d) nose

49. As 'accept' is related to 'refuse', similarly 'hide' is related to
(a) allow (b) reveal
(c) observe (d) hear

50. As 'teacher' is related to 'instruction', similarly 'musician' is related to
(a) music (b) songs
(c) entertainment (d) opera

CHAPTER 12

Jumbled Words and Jumbled Sentences

To jumble means mixing things in a confusing manner. The jumbled words exercise includes changing the order of the letters of a word and it tests a child's vocabulary. The jumbled sentences exercise teaches the child sentence formation.

e.g. (Jumbled words) ONMYEK = Monkey
ABVER = Brave

e.g. (Jumbled sentence)

milk/gives/milkman/us
Milkman gives us milk.

Let's Practice

Directions (Q. Nos. 1-10) Some words are given below in a jumbled manner. Arrange them in a proper order.

1. ROWOMORT

2. DLIOAYH

3. LRBIARY

4. TALBFLOO

5. CHETIKN

6. KCHIENC

7. AOBDR

8. PUMCORET

9. TCRODO

10. RSCUCI

Directions (Q. Nos. 11-24) Given below are sentences in which words are jumbled. Arrange them to form meaningful sentences.

11. the/ first/ doctor/ a/ diagnosis/ makes/ an/ illness/ of
(a) Diagnosis the doctor makes first of an illness.
(b) The doctor first makes a diagnosis of an illness.
(c) First the diagnosis of an illness the doctor makes.
(d) The diagnosis first of an illness the doctor makes.

12. he/ or she/ what/ then/ kind/ decides/ of treatment/ needed/ is
(a) She or he then what kind of treatment is needed decides.
(b) He or she decides what kind of treatment then needed.
(c) Then he or she decides what kind of treatment is needed.
(d) What kind of treatment is needed then he or she decides.

13. can/ treated/ with/ many/ be/ a/ course/ of/ drugs/ illnesses
(a) Many illnesses with a course of drugs can be treated.
(b) Can be treated many illnesses with a course of drugs.
(c) Many illnesses can be treated with a course of drugs.
(d) Illness many can be treated with a course of drugs.

14. may/ the doctor/ if/ is/ serious/ the/ case/ operate
(a) Operate may the doctor if the serious is the case.
(b) The doctor may operate if the case is serious.
(c) The doctor may operate serious case if is .
(d) If the case is serious the doctor operate may.

15. one/ respect/ doctor's/ must/ always/ opinion/the
(a) Must the respect always one doctor's opinion
(b) Respect one the must always doctor's opinion
(c) One respect must always doctor's the opinion.
(d) One must always respect the doctor's opinion.

16. necessary/ are/ growth/of/ sports/ for/ body/ the
(a) For the body growth of sports are necessary.
(b) Sports are necessary for growth of the body.
(c) Necessary are sports for growth of the body.
(d) The growth of body are necessary for sports.

17. body/ keep/ the/ fresh/ and/ they/ fit
(a) Fit and fresh they keep the body
(b) Fresh and they keep the body fit.
(c) They keep the body fresh and fit.
(d) Keep they the body fit and fresh.

18. give/ exercise/ to/ they/ whole/ body/ the
(a) They give exercise to the whole body.
(b) Give they exercise to the whole body.
(c) Whole body they give exercise to.
(d) Exercise they give to the whole body.

19. developing/ not only/ sports/ a/ mind/ but also/ help/ in/ his/ body/ child's
(a) Sports help but also in developing his mind not only child's body
(b) Help sports in not only in developing child's body but also his mind.
(c) Sports help not only in developing a child's body but also his mind.
(d) In developing but also mind body not only a child's sports help his.

20. have/ first/ in/ I/ prize/ competition/ won/ the/ cooking
(a) In cooking competition the first prize I have won.
(b) I have won first prize in the cooking competition.
(c) I won cooking competition have in first prize the.
(d) I have won cooking competition in the first prize.

21. the/ love/ weekend/ I
(a) The weekend love I.
(b) I love the weekend.
(c) I weekend the love.
(d) None of these

22. finish/ work/ early/ one/ can/ go/ and/ a/ for walk/ one's
(a) Work can finish and one early go for a walk one's.
(b) One's go for a work and can finish one walk early.
(c) One can finish one's work early and go for a walk.
(d) Finish one can one's work early and go for a walk.

23. bats/ are/ most/ to people/ harmless
(a) Most bats are harmless to people.
(b) Bats most are harmless to people.
(c) People are most harmless to bats.
(d) Most harmless are bats to people.

24. on/ Mohit/ skating/ and/ Saturday/ Preeti/ went/ for
(a) On Saturday Mohit and Preeti skating went for.
(b) Mohit and Preeti went for skating on Saturday.
(c) On Saturday for skating Mohit and Preeti went.
(d) Saturday Mohit and Preeti on for skating went.

Directions (Q. Nos. 25-27) The parts of each sentence have been jumbled and are marked as P, Q, R and S. Rearrange the parts to form the sentence correctly and select the correct option accordingly.

25. everyone (P)/follow (Q)/should (R)/traffic rules (S)

(a) P R S Q (b) P R Q S
(c) R P S Q (d) None of these

26. God (P)/ in distress only (Q)/ some people (R)/ remember (S)

(a) P Q R S (b) Q P R S (c) R S P Q (d) S R P Q

27. want me (P)/ at the airport (Q)/ do you (R)/ to see you off (S)

(a) Q P R S (b) R P S Q (c) Q R P S (d) R S Q P

Directions (Q. Nos. 28-37) In the story given below, select the correct words to fill the blanks marked by numbers from the option given.

Once there was a king who had an elephant. The elephant's trainer took it to a river for a bath ...(28).... It always passed by a tailor's shop in the ...(29).... The tailor used to feed ...(30)... to the elephant.

One day the tailor was in a ...(31)... mood. When the elephant came as usual to his shop, the tailor pricked its trunk with a ...(32).... This annoyed the elephant, but it went away...(33)....

After ...(34)... its bath in the river, the elephant filled his trunk with muddy water. When it passed by the tailor's shop, it ...(35)... the muddy water all over the new clothes ...(36)... by the tailor. Thus, all the new ...(37)... got soiled.

28. (a) dayevery (b) everyady
(c) everyday (d) yardevey

29. (a) kartem (b) market
(c) karmet (d) matker

30. (a) nanabas (b) nabanas
(c) bananas (d) sananab

31. (a) fullpay (b) playful
(c) payfull (d) layflup

32. (a) needel (b) nedlee
(c) needle (d) endlee

33. (a) lequity (b) equitly
(c) quitely (d) quietly

34. (a) completing (b) compliteng
(c) clompiteng (d) clemptoing

35. (a) quirsted (b) quitsred
(c) squitred (d) squirted

36. (a) stichetd (b) tistedch
(c) stitched (d) stitchde

37. (a) slothec (b) ostchel
(c) clothes (d) clothse

Directions (Q. Nos. 38-47) In each of the following questions, arrange the four parts of the sentence given below in the correct order to make a meaningful sentence and select the correct option accordingly.

38. A. him to life
B. Rohit can't carry
C. It's too heavy for
D. this suitcase because

(a) B A D C (b) C B D A
(c) B D C A (d) A D B C

39. A. comfortable to live in
B. house as it was very
C. both loved their small
D. Rakesh and Ameeta

(a) D B C A (b) D C B A
(c) A B C D (d) A B D C

40. A. in the morning
B. by the housemaid
C. all the rooms are
D. cleaned and swept

(a) DCBA (b) BADC (c) BCDA (d) CDBA

41. A. a cash prize for
B. to his surprise,
C. catching the thief
D. Praveen was given

(a) BDAC (b) BDCA (c) CDAB (d) ACDB

42. A. do your friends
B. afternoon every day
C. playground in the
D. play in the

(a) ADBC (b) CBDA (c) DCBA (d) ADCB

43. A. the lion is
B. the jungle
C. known as the
D. king of
(a) BCAD (b) CDBA (c) CDAB (d) ACDB

44. A. bus because she
B. arrives late at her stop
C. Raveena sometimes
D. misses the school
(a) CABD (b) CDAB (c) BCAD (d) ABDC

45. A. poverty in India
B. be done by the
C. a lot of work must
D. government to reduce
(a) ACDB (b) CBAD (c) CBDA (d) DBAC

46. A. please carry the
B. cooked dishes to
C. the dining room
D. Salim, could you
(a) DCBA (b) ABCD (c) DABC (d) BCAD

47. A. spoken in China
B. many characters
C. in the Mandarin language
D. there are too
(a) DBCA (b) ADCB (c) BCDA (d) CADB

Directions (Q. Nos. 48-50) In each of the following questions, a passage is given with the first and last sentences identified as A and Z. The remaining four sentence are labelled as P, Q, R and S. Find the correct sequence of these four sentences and select the correct option accordingly.

48. A. A number of great women of India have their names written with golden letters in the history books of India.
P. After a son has born to the young princess, tragedy struck the royal household.
Q. She was born of a poor family but was married to the son of Malharrao Holkar, the great Maratha Chief, who ruled over Malwa in the middle of the 18th century.
R. Rani Ahalyabai is one such lady.
S. Both Malharrao and his son were killed in a battle.
Z. Thus, Ahalyabai was called upon to take up the reins of her state at a very early age.
(a) RQPS (b) QPSR
(c) RPSQ (d) RSQP

49. A. A lemming is a very unusual animal found in very cold parts of the world.
P. They jump in and start swimming and they keep swimming, until at last they are so tired that they have to stop swimming.
Q. And then, of course, they drown.
R. They cross fields and woods and they swim across streams and rivers, until after several months of travelling, they reach the sea.
S. Once in every few years, the lemmings leave their homes in the mountains and start travelling.
Z. Hundreds and thousands of lemmings drown in this fashion.
(a) RSQP (b) SPRQ
(c) RPQS (d) SRPQ

50. A. Hibernation is more than sleep.
P. The first is that it stores a lot of fat in its body during summer and autumn.
Q. It is a very deep sleep.
R. The answer lies in two facts.
S. Hibernating in this way, the animal can sleep all through the winter without eating for many months.
Z. The second is related to the main use the body makes of food-to supply the energy for movement.
(a) SQRP (b) PQRS
(c) QSRP (d) PRQS

Synonyms

Word	Synonyms
Awkward	rough, ungainly or clumsy
Apathy	unconcern, aloofness
Alien	outsider, foreigner
Antique	old fashioned, ancient
Blemish	fault, stigma
Blame	censure, reproach
Contrary	conflicting, opposite
Contempt	disregard, scorn
Calm	quiet, mild, peaceful
Careful	alert, cautious
Consent	agree, permit
Capable	suitable, competent, qualified
Delicious	tasty, palatable, appetising
Dedicate	devote, loyal, surrender
Exempt	excuse, release, absolve
Evident	apparent, obvious, clear
Esteem	respect, regards, reverence

Word	Synonyms
Enormous	immense, mammoth
Fragile	weak, frail
Foe	enemy, opponent, adversary
Fantasy	imagination, image, vision
Fabulous	grand, remarkable
Glow	shine, shimmer
Harmful	hurtful, injurious
Hamper	hinder, obstruct
Indulge	gratify, pamper, confront
Incite	provoke, arouse
Immense	huge, enormous, gigantic
Judicious	thoughtful, prudent
Jubilant	cheerful, rejoicing
Lucid	coherent, sound
Liberate	rescue, emancipate
Modest	humble, reserved
Miraculous	extraordinary, amazing

Let's Practice

Directions (Q. Nos. 1-10) Find the suitable synonym for the underlined word in the sentences from the given options.

1. It is very difficult to understand a foreign language.
(a) simple (b) challenging
(c) tricky (d) easy

2. This toy is inexpensive.
(a) overpriced (b) expensive
(c) cheap (d) good

3. He never reaches on time.
(a) sees (b) arrives (c) does (d) goes

4. Do you think I am stupid?
(a) foolish (b) intelligent
(c) brilliant (d) fast

5. He is a fast runner.
(a) slow (b) energetic (c) calm (d) quick

6. I am terrible at Mathematics.
(a) awful (b) good (c) great (d) slow

7. The music is very loud.
(a) soft (b) catchy (c) awesome (d) blaring

8. I require five big speakers.
(a) demand (b) need (c) found (d) got

9. My sister is very pretty.
(a) strange (b) ugly (c) beautiful (d) dotty

10. The students were confused over the time table issue.
(a) agitated (b) exhausted
(c) settle (d) baffled

Directions (Q. Nos. 11-20) In each of the following questions, select the option which is a synonym of the given word.

11. Weak
(a) sapped (b) frail (c) strong (d) hefty

12. Small
(a) short (b) fine (c) tiny (d) flimsy

13. Alert
(a) smart (b) watchful (c) rustic (d) live

14. Faith
(a) proof (b) believe
(c) repose (d) agree

15. Alien
(a) occupant (b) native
(c) foreigner d) emigrant

16. Blame
(a) praise (b) appreciate
(c) criticise (d) command

17. Consent
(a) agree (b) permission
(c) disagree (d) object

18. Disaster
(a) happiness (b) lively
(c) mishap (d) auspicious

19. Foe
(a) helper (b) comrade (c) enemy (d) helper

20. Hail
(a) greet (b) avoid (c) awful (d) honour

Directions (Q. Nos. 21-30) In each question, one option is different from the others. Find the odd one out.

21. (a) Homely (b) Plain (c) Refined (d) Simple

22. (a) Fragile (b) Tough (c) Weak (d) Infirm

23. (a) Run (b) Gallop (c) Sit (d) Dash

24. (a) Launch (b) Keep (c) Propel (d) Shoot

25. (a) Busy (b) Quiet (c) Occupied (d) Active

26. (a) Clever (b) Stupid
(c) Cunning (d) Crafty

27. (a) Grief (b) Sorrow
(c) Joy (d) Distress

28. (a) Worship (b) Devotion
(c) Disrespect (d) Dedication

29. (a) Fame (b) Dishonour
(c) Esteem (d) Prestige

30. (a) Afraid (b) Frightened
(c) Scared (d) Composed

31. Match the words in List I with their synonyms in List II.

	List I		List II
A.	Folly	1.	Fit
B.	Shelter	2.	Frightened
C.	Suitable	3.	Mistake
D.	Afraid	4.	Cover

Codes

	A	B	C	D		A	B	C	D
(a)	2	1	3	4	(b)	4	1	2	3
(c)	3	4	1	2	(d)	3	2	4	1

32. Replace the underlined words in List I with their synonyms in List II.

	List I		List II
A.	My mother is <u>educated</u>.	1.	habit
B.	Jubin is pointed out for his <u>uncouth</u> manners.	2.	dismissed
C.	The boy was <u>fired</u> for coming to school late everyday.	3.	ungracious
D.	It was his <u>practice</u> to go for a walk every morning.	4.	literate

Codes

	A	B	C	D		A	B	C	D
(a)	3	2	4	1	(b)	4	3	1	2
(c)	4	3	2	1	(d)	3	1	2	4

Directions (Q. Nos. 33-37) Read the passage carefully and answer the questions that follow.

The most beautiful humming birds are <u>found</u> in the West Indies and South America. The crest of the <u>tiny</u> head of one of these shines like a <u>sparkling</u> crown of coloured light. The shades of colour that <u>adorn</u> its breast are equally brilliant. As the bird flits from one object to another, it looks more like a bright flash of sunlight than it does like a <u>living</u> being.

33. Choose the synonym of the word found used in the passage.

(a) begin (b) caught sight of
(c) establish (d) considered

34. Find the synonym of the word tiny used in the passage.

(a) huge (b) small
(c) prominent (d) vast

35. Choose the correct synonym of the word sparkling in the passage.

(a) shining (b) dull
(c) dark (d) gloomy

36. Replace the word adorn in the passage with a suitable synonym.

(a) spoil (b) reduce (c) hurt (d) decorate

37. Find out the synonym of the word living used in the passage.

(a) lifeless (b) dull (c) alive (d) inactive

Directions (Q. Nos. 38-45) Select the synonym of the given word and complete the crossword.

38. Eat

(a) Lunch (b) Munch (c) Adapt (d) Amaze

39. Run

(a) Gallop (b) Sprint (c) Demist (d) Compel

40. Hop

(a) Flow (b) Pull (c) Jump (d) Draw

41. Stone

(a) Foul (b) Sand (c) Rock (d) Dune

42. Throw

(a) Hack (b) Toss (c) Keep (d) Gulp

43. Talk

(a) Leave (b) Sneak
(c) Laugh (d) Speak

44. Huge

(a) Loyal (b) Giant
(c) Melody (d) Lower

45. Fire

(a) Match (b) Flame
(c) Stick (d) Shoot

Antonyms

An antonym is a word which means opposite of the given word. e.g. 'stop' has its antonym as 'go'.

Word	Antonyms
Aversion	affection, fondness
Affront	mollify, appease
Assert	reject, conceal
Accord	dissent, withhold
Abate	aggravate, intensify
Brittle	slown, flexible
Blemish	purity, spotless
Benevolence	unkindness, malevolence
Compassion	cruelty, apathy
Consequence	source, cause
Caress	repulse, spurn
Disaster	prosperity, happiness
Demolish	repair, construct
Deliberate	rash, sudden
Heavy	light, easy
Exempt	confine, enforce
Evade	confront, verify
Frivolous	solemn, essential
Fluent	hesitant, slow
Fickle	resolute, determined
Fabulous	historical, mediocre

Word	Antonyms
Gloom	delight, joviality
Generous	miserly, stingy
Hideous	attractive, splendid
Hamper	promote, foster
Intimidate	console, encourage
Intrigue	sincerity, honesty
Indulge	annoy, trouble
Impartial	prejudiced, unjust
Justify	impute, accuse
Luscious	bland, distasteful
Lavish	conserve, frugal
Lament	amuse, entertain
Modest	brave, intricate
Mitigate	augment, enhance
Novice	expert, experienced
Negligent	vigilant, careful
Offspring	ancestors, forefathers
Obstruct	hasten, encourage
Prudent	reckless, unwise
Profuse	scarce, meagre
Rustic	cultured, refined

Let's Practice

Directions (Q. Nos. 1-10) Choose the suitable antonym for the underlined word in the sentence.

1. The measurements were absolutely <u>accurate</u>.
(a) exact (b) precise
(c) inaccurate (d) correct

2. Silk does not <u>shrink</u> like other fabrics.
(a) bright (b) expire (c) expand (d) excuse

3. <u>Fertile</u> soil is required for growing crops.
(a) barren (b) fudge
(c) productive (d) lush

4. He <u>vanished</u> without a trace.
(a) disappeared (b) appeared
(c) approved (d) rejected

5. The goalkeeper's mistake resulted in <u>defeat</u> for the team.
(a) loss (b) conquer (c) victory (d) treat

6. The manager wanted to meet the trainees in <u>private</u>.
(a) house (b) slow (c) more (d) public

7. The flight <u>arrived</u> at 6 o' clock in the evening.
(a) safe (b) begin
(c) succeed (d) departed

8. The climate of Sahara is very <u>harsh</u>.
(a) cruel (b) severe
(c) pleasant (d)cold

9. I am an <u>optimist</u>.
(a) nervous (b) pessimist
(c) arrogant (d) intelligent

10. One should <u>avoid</u> late night jobs.
(a) inspire (b) compel
(c) pursue (d) do

Directions (Q. Nos. 11-20) In each of the following questions, select the option which is an antonym of the word given.

11. Mean
(a) Happy (b) Tall (c) Weird (d) Nice

12. Strong
(a) Thin (b) Young (c) Weak (d) Light

13. Together
(a) Alone (b) Light (c) Crowded (d) Heavy

14. Difficult
(a) Soft (b) Old (c) Easy (d) Hard

15. Stern
(a) Serious (b) Lenient (c) Carefree (d) Neat

16. Rare
(a) Painful (b) Creepy (c) Normal (d) Common

17. Lead
(a) Direct (b) Help (c) Follow (d) Manage

18. Enter
(a) Come (b) Exit (c) Celebrate (d) Join

19. Remove
(a) Peel (b) Burn (c) Stir (d) Add

20. Loud
(a) Noisy (b) Quiet (c) Sick (d) Hard

Directions (Q. Nos. 21-30) In these question, one option is different from others. Choose the odd one out.

21. (a) Sad (b) Unhappy (c) Gloomy (d) Joyful

22. (a) Dispute (b) Debate
(c) Discuss (d) Agree

23. (a) Criticise (b) Praise
(c) Blame (d) Accuse

24. (a) Propel (b) Activate
(c) Halt (d) Energise

25. (a) Dislike (b) Loathe
(c) Reject (d) Cherish

26. (a) Rarely (b) Always
(c) Often (d) Usually

27. (a) Reply (b) Solution
(c) Answer (d) Happening

28. (a) Careful (b) Indifferent
(c) Attentive (d) Watchful

29. (a) Timid (b) Shy
(c) Confident (d) Reserved

30. (a) Sunny (b) Bright
(c) Clear (d) Dim

Directions (Q. Nos. 31-35) In the following questions, add the prefix to make the word its antonym.

31. Agree
(a) In (b) Un (c) Dis (d) Im

32. Possible
(a) Un (b) Im (c) In (d) Un

33. Able
(a) Pre (b) Non (c) Im (d) Un

34. Legal
(a) Un (b) Il (c) Im (d) Un

35. Qualify
(a) Un (b) Im (c) Dis (d) Non

36. Match the words in List I with their antonyms in List II.

List I		List II	
A.	Sweet	1.	Calm
B.	Windy	2.	Happy
C.	Scared	3.	Bitter
D.	Upset	4.	Bold

Codes

	A	B	C	D		A	B	C	D
(a)	2	1	3	4	(b)	3	2	1	4
(c)	3	1	4	2	(d)	4	3	1	2

37. Choose the antonym of the underlined word in List I from List II.

List I		List II	
A.	Red light says, "stop".	1.	hatred
B.	Homework sometimes is very boring.	2.	unavailable
C.	The books are available at the school shop.	3.	go
D.	Children should be treated with love.	4.	interesting

Codes

	A	B	C	D		A	B	C	D
(a)	2	1	3	4	(b)	3	4	2	1
(c)	4	1	2	3	(d)	1	4	3	2

Directions (Q. Nos. 38-43) Read the passage given below and choose the antonym of the underlined words from the options.

The doctor is a person who looks after sick ...(38)... people and prescribes medicine so that the patients recover fast ...(39)... In order to become a doctor, a person has to study medicine. Doctors lead a hard ...(40)... life. Their life is very busy ...(41)... They get up early in the morning and go to the hospital. They work without taking a break. They always remain polite ...(42)... so that the patients feel comfortable ...(43)... with them. Since doctors work so hard we must realise their value.

38. (a) old (b) healthy
(c) unhealthy (d) slow

39. (a) steady (b) slow
(c) quick (d) immediately

40. (a) difficult (b) strenuous
(c) easy (d) comfort

41. (a) happy (b) idle
(c) relaxed (d) engaged

42. (a) rude (b) strange (c) civil (d) cordial

43. (a) easy (b) unpleasant
(c) uncomfortable (d) useful

Directions (Q. Nos. 44-50) Select the antonym of the given words.

44. Smooth
(a) Soft (b) Big (c) Large (d) Rough

45. Dull
(a) Dark (b) Burning (c) Colourful (d) High

46. Low
(a) Small (b) Slow (c) Huge (d) High

47. Soft
(a) Hot (b) Noisy (c) Little (d) Hard

48. Smile
(a) Cry (b) Laugh (c) Frown (d) Sad

49. Big
(a) Small (b) Tiny (c) Little (d) Few

50. Go
(a) Come (b) Walk (c) Run (d) Talk

Short Composition

Short compositions are meant to improve a child's writing skill and creativity. They consist of different writing forms.

1. **Notice** It is written text to inform the people in a simple and precise manner about an event or an activity. It is used by both individuals and organisations.

Format of a Notice

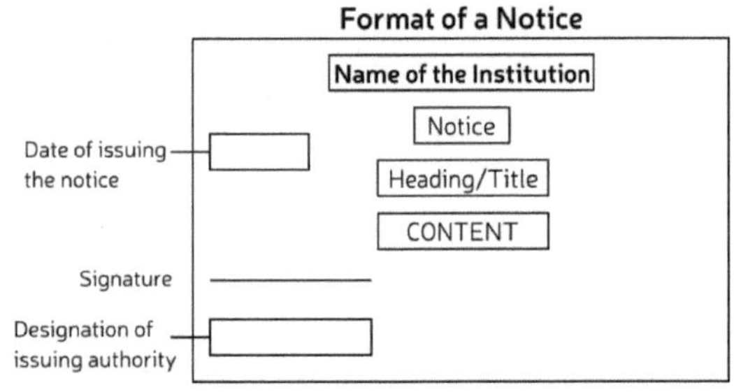

2. **Message** A message is written or sent to convey information to a person who is not present at that moment.

Format of a Message

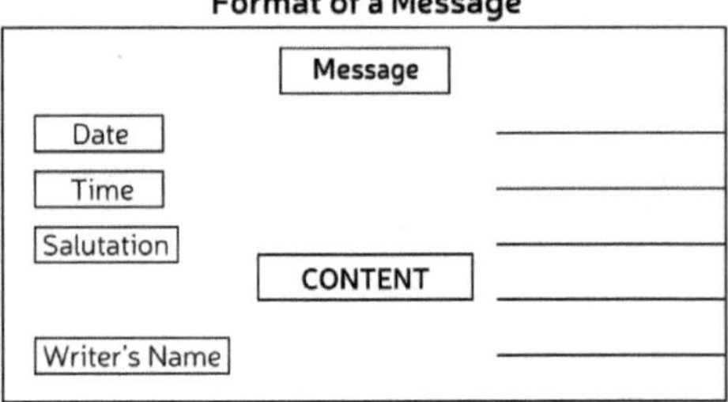

3. **Story Writing** It is an imaginary piece of writing to improve the creativity of a student. It can be developed with the help of pictures or verbal hints.

4. **Letter Writing** It is a written or typed form of communication conveying information (in the case of an informal letter) or requesting an authority for something (in the case of a letter to the Principal, for instance).

Format of an Informal Letter

1. Sender's Address
   Flat no. 503, Hyber Heights, Hyderabad
2. Date : 10th August, 20xx
3. (Salutation) Dear Mark
4. (Body of the letter)
   ______(para 1)______
   ______(para 2)______
   ______(para 3)______
   ______(para 4)______
5. (Subscription) with love
6. Name

Let's Practice

Directions (Q.Nos. 1-7) Format of a notice is given below in which different parts are numbered. Identify the numbers by choosing the correct option.

4
7
3
2
5
6
1

1. The item identified as 1 is ....
   (a) heading (b) notice
   (c) designation of the issuer (d) date

2. The item identified as 2 is ....
   (a) name of the organisation
   (b) subject of the notice
   (c) subject matter of the notice
   (d) date of the notice

3. The item identified as 3 is ....
   (a) subject of the notice
   (b) name of issuing organisation
   (c) the word 'Notice'
   (d) date of notice

4. The item identified as 4 is ....
   (a) designation of the issuer of the notice
   (b) name of the institution/organisation
   (c) subject of the notice
   (d) date of the notice

5. The item identified as 5 is ....
   (a) date of the notice (b) content of the notice
   (c) subject of the notice (d) issuer's signature

6. The item identified as 6 is ....
   (a) signature of issuer (b) date of the notice
   (c) contents of the notice (d) name of organisation

7. The item identified as 7 is ....
   (a) the word 'Notice'
   (b) subject of the notice
   (c) date of the notice
   (d) name of the organisation

Directions (Q.Nos. 8-12) A notice is given below with some missing parts numbered 8 to 12. The question of the notice is given below so that notice is understood.

(You are Secretary of Environment club of Manav Rachna School, Faridabad. A notice is to be written on your behalf informing students of a tree plantation drive to celebrate 'Van Mahotsav Day'.)

......(8)......

Notice

3rd July, 2015

Tree Plantation Drive

All students of classes 6 to 12 are hereby informed that a ....(9)....... will be held in the school campus on 6th July, 2015 at 10 : 30 A.M. Each Child's ....(10)....... is mandatory. Each class has to bring minimum five tree ....(11)....... . The aim of this drive is to make our environment clean and green and celebrate this day as Van Mahotsav day.

Nitin Kathuria

.......(12)....... .

8. The item identified as 8 is ....
   (a) the word notice
   (b) Manav Rachna School, Faridabad
   (c) Van Mahotsav day
   (d) tree plantation

9. The item identified as 9 is ....
   (a) environment club meeting
   (b) Van Mahotsav day
   (c) tree plantation drive
   (d) function

10. The item identified as 10 is ....
   (a) presence
   (b) attendance
   (c) contribution
   (d) function

11. The item identified as 11 is ....

(a) branches
(b) plants
(c) saplings
(d) trees

12. The item identified as 12 is ....

(a) Cultural Secretary
(b) Principal
(c) Chairman
(d) Secretary Environment Club

Directions (Q. Nos. 13-17) A message is given below in which different parts are numbered. Identify the number by choosing the correct option.

	15
16	
17	
	13
14	

13. The item identified as 13 is ....

(a) The word 'Message'
(b) Content
(c) Name of the writer
(d) Date

14. The item identified as 14 is ....

(a) date of the message
(b) the word 'message'
(c) subject matter of the message
(d) name of the person who has written the message

15. The item identified as 15 is ....

(a) the content
(b) name of person
(c) the word 'Message'
(d) date of message

16. The item identified as 16 is ....

(a) the word 'Message'
(b) name of writer
(c) date of the message
(d) time of message

17. The item identified as 17 is ....

(a) salutation
(b) date of message
(c) main message
(d) time of message

Directions (Q. Nos. 18-23) You receive a telephone call from your mother's office when she is not at home. You have the following conversation with the speaker. You have to go for your tuition class before your mother returns home. So you leave a message for your mother. Fill in the numbered blanks in the message given below by selecting the appropriate option.

Ambuj: Hello!

Mr Rastogi: Hello! May I speak to Mrs. Dixit please? I am Naresh Rastogi from the office.

Ambuj: Mom's not at home right now.

Mr Rastogi: In that case, can you give her a message? It is urgent. Please tell her that the meeting fixed for tomorrow has been rescheduled. Ask her to check her mail as soon as possible for the details. Please don't forget to inform her.

Ambuj: Don't worry. I will tell her as soon as she returns.

> ......(18)......
>
> 14th July
> 3:30 P.M.
> Mom
>
> Mr Rastogi from the ....(19)....... called up to say that the ....(20)....... fixed for tomorrow has been ....(21)....... . He wants you to ....(22)....... your mail as soon as possible for the details. He said it was ....(23)....... .
>
> Ambuj

18. (a) Notice (b) Application (c) Message (d) Subject

19. (a) home (b) conference room (c) office (d) market

20. (a) meeting (b) appointment (c) interview (d) conference

21. (a) postponed (b) preponed (c) rescheduled (d) cancelled

22. (a) send (b) check (c) see (d) draft

23. (a) important (b) emergency (c) urgent (d) critical

Directions (Q. Nos. 24-30) Read the story carefully and answer the questions that follow.

There was an old man living in his village. He had four sons and they were very lazy. The old man fell sick and was ....(24)....... his last days in bed. He worried a lot about his sons' future as the young men hesitated to work. The sons believed that luck would favour them.

The old man's health deteriorated every day and he decided to talk to his sons about their future. However, his sons did not listen to him. The old man ......(25)...... to let his sons realise the importance of work.

He called all his sons and let them sit near him an his bed. He said he had a treasure box with gold coins and expensive gems for them and wanted to share the treasure equally and lead a happy, prosperous life. The young men were very happy and asked where their father had placed the ......(26)...... . The old man replied, 'I cannot exactly remember the place where I had hidden the treasure from the others. However, the treasure box is buried in our land. I'm really not sure about the place where I had .....(27).....'.

Even though the lazy young sons were happy, they were sad that the old man forgot the place where the treasure was hidden. After a few days, the old man died. The sons decided ......(28)...... to find the treasure box.

After sometime, they realised that it was the hard work that was mentioned as 'Treasure Box' by their father. They forgot their laziness, worked hard, earned money and lived happily.

24. (a) nearing (b) approaching (c) counting (d) measuring

25. (a) played a game (b) played a tune (c) played music (d) played a trick

26. (a) money (b) treasure (c) coins (d) gems

27. (a) lost the treasure box
(b) covered the treasure box
(c) hidden the treasure box
(d) wrapped the treasure box

28. (a) to uncover the land (b) to dig the land (c) to locate the land (d) look for the land

29. What was mentioned as 'treasure box' by the father?
(a) A box containing lots of coins
(b) Hard work
(c) Continued search
(d) Unity among the sons

30. What can be a suitable title of this story?
(a) Old man and his lazy sons
(b) The treasure box
(c) Hard work is the best treasure
(d) Lazy boys and the treasure box

Directions (Q. Nos. 31-40) An informal letter is given below. Complete it by filling the blanks.

17 L1C Apartments
Lucknow -226001
.......(31).......
.......(32)....... Jazzy,

Many thanks for your letter and photographs. They brought back very happy memories of our holiday. Indeed the time spent ....(33)....... has ended up being one of the best I have had so far. India is full of fascinating ....(34)....... and your company was really wonderful. In future more such ....(35)....... should be planned. Do let me know when you are planning to visit my place. What a joy it would be to ....(36)....... and have you amongst us.

Catch you later
.......(37).......
Michael

31. (a) Pincode (b) time (c) name of state (d) 3rd July, 20xx

32. (a) Respectfully (b) Dear (c) Hi (d) Lovely

33. (a) with you (b) alone (c) together (d) family

34. (a) locations (b) cities (c) places (d) resorts

35. (a) outings (b) trips (c) picnics (d) meetings

36. (a) meeting (b) seeing (c) see you (d) talk to you

37. (a) Hi (b) Bye (c) Missing you (d) Yours faithfully

Reading Comprehension

Comprehension is the basic purpose of reading any form of written text. It is the ability to read and understand meaning of the text.

The process of comprehension involves making sense of words, connecting ideas expressed in the text and relating ideas with one's knowledge.

For better comprehension, a well developed vocabulary as well as prior knowledge is required, in addition to ability to make inferences.

Let's Practice

Directions (Passage I-VI) Read the passages carefully and answer the questions that follow.

Passage I

To the children, the park seemed to be shrinking. Cass could remember when the paddock at the bottom of the valley had been full of bushes and long yellow grass. Great for playing hidey in. Now it was gone.

First came the two high squat blocks of units that hid the early winter Sun. Within an year, what was left of the tall grass was covered by identical red brick town houses. The paddock had disappeared.

Trumper Park was their island in the middle of the city noise. The Trumper Tree grew in the centre of the park half-way up the hill, its great grey branches spreading wide, its leaves changing from olive-green to yellow-gold as the year grew older.

Mrs Valchase hated that tree. Its leaves blew into her walled garden. The fruit bats that made it their home were much too noisy. And now she'd applied to the council to have it cut down.

The Becketts and their neighbours had formed a residents' committee to save the tree, but their negotiations with the overbearing Mrs Valchase had failed. She insisted the tree be cut down. 'It blocks my view,' she claimed.

The grass looked green and inviting under the Trumper Tree. Cass threw herself down in the shade, stretching her arms and legs on the cool grass. Lying like this, she gazed into the spreading canopy of branches. Dark green leaves patchworked with blue sky drifted and changed with the breeze, dappled sunlight flecking the ancient grey roots. 'It really is a special tree. Mum's right, it does seem to know everything.'

'You talk as if the tree is a person, Cass.' Carl bit into a sandwich and Cass stretched out her hand for one.

'I suppose I do a bit. But I can't imagine it not being there. What are we going to do? We must do something.'

Carl sat chewing, his glasses balanced on the very tip of his nose. One more chew and they would slip off. 'Well', Carl lifted his head and his glasses slid back into place, 'I don't know if we can do anything more, Cass. If adults can't stop them, what can we do?'

1. 'The park seemed to be shrinking'. Why did the children feel or say this?
   (a) The park was overcrowded
   (b) Part of the park was occupied
   (c) The park was gradually being replaced by buildings
   (d) The favourite tree of the children was being cut down

2. 'Trumper Park was their island in the middle of the city noise'. This means that the park ....
   (a) occupied a central location in the city
   (b) was situated at the noisiest part of the city
   (c) had a paddock to relax
   (d) was a much desired place away from the noise of the city

3. Which word in the 5th paragraph supports the view that Mrs Valchase is overbearing?
   (a) failed (b) insisted
   (c) claimed (d) blocks

4. The word 'canopy' in the 6th paragraph would mean ....
   (a) umbrella (b) covering
   (c) floor (d) jungle

5. An antonym of the word 'spreading' used in the 3rd paragraph is
   (a) smudging (b) folding
   (c) moving (d) streaking

Passage II

A tornado is a tight, funnel-shaped column of spinning air. The speed of spin increases as its diameter narrows. Within the funnel, air pressure is so low that the difference in pressure inside the funnel and outside it can make a building <u>explode</u> if a tornado passes over it.

Tornadoes are amazing as much as they are terrifying. A tornado can rip trees out by their roots, derail trains and sweep people, animals and even small buildings into the air. But, particularly in the case of people and animals, the tornado can land them back safely on Earth and completely unharmed. On 29th May, 1986, 12 school children were sucked up by a tornado in Western China. They were found on some sand dunes some 20 km away after the tornado had passed, perfectly safe.

A tornado can create much damage but the area it wrecks is quite small. The path of greatest destruction thus far recorded is rarely more than 100 metres wide. Because of this fact, a tornado can cause total destruction to a house on one side of a street while leaving a house on the opposite side untouched.

It is difficult to measure the exact speed of wind in the centre of a tornado as monitoring equipment can never survive the <u>onslaught</u>. It has been estimated that the speed of wind there is about 400 km/h. Whatever it is, a consolation is that tornadoes are short-lived-dying out usually within an hour or two.

1. Spinning air inside a tornado increases in speed when ....
   (a) the funnel's diameter expands
   (b) the air pressure reduces
   (c) the funnel's diameter decreases
   (d) the air pressure of outside and inside becomes equal

2. How can tornadoes be amazing? It can be when ....
   (a) it causes millions of deaths
   (b) it leaves much debris on Earth
   (c) it causes much destruction
   (d) it can bring back man and animals on Earth safe and unharmed.

3. The tornado may cause a building to explode because of ....
   (a) its strength
   (b) difference in air pressure between its inside and outside
   (c) its duration
   (d) the force in its column of spinning air

4. A synonym of the word 'explode' as used in 1st paragraph is ....
   (a) rage
   (b) escalate
   (c) burst violently
   (d) ridicule

5. The word 'onslaught' in the last paragraph would mean ....
   (a) a large number of people or things
   (b) assault
   (c) retreat
   (d) charge

Passage III

Butterflies are some of the most interesting insects on the planet Earth. There are more than seventeen thousand different kinds of butterflies! Butterflies come in all shapes and sizes.

Butterflies go through four main stages of life. The first stage is the egg stage, followed by the larva stage. As a larva, or caterpillar, the future butterfly eats as much as possible. As it grows, it sheds its outer skin, or exoskeleton. This may happen four or five times. After a few weeks, the caterpillar enters the next stage of its life, the chrysalis stage. In the chrysalis, the caterpillar will liquify into a soup of living cells. Then, it will reorganise into a butterfly and the metamorphosis is complete. In later parts of the chrysalis stage, you can see the forming butterfly through the chrysalis.

When the butterfly emerges from the chrysalis, it pumps its wings to send blood through them so that it can fly. Most butterflies only live a couple of weeks, just enough time to drink flower nectar and to mate. Some, like the Monarch butterfly, however, may live many months.

1. Which of the following is not true?
   (a) Butterflies must wait until blood drains into their wings before flying
   (b) The butterfly may shed its skin 10 to 12 times
   (c) Caterpillars liquifies into a soup of living cells
   (d) Most butterflies live for weeks, at the most for a few months

2. The second stage of life of a butterfly is ....
   (a) larva
   (b) egg
   (c) chrysalis
   (d) butterfly

3. Which of the following statements is true?
   (a) There are about a thousand different kinds of butterflies in the world
   (b) There are more than seventeen thousand different kinds of butterflies
   (c) There are only a few hundred different kinds of butterflies
   (d) There is only one kind of butterfly in the world

4. The word 'metamorphosis' used in 2nd paragraph of the passage would mean ....
   (a) translation
   (b) transformation
   (c) stagnation
   (d) adjustment

5. Find the antonym of the word 'emerges' given in the last paragraph.
   (a) appears (b) reveals
   (c) disappears (d) rises

Passage IV

Venus is sometimes called Earth's sister planet, though its similarities with Earth are limited, apart from size and relative condition of its surface. It is easily observed with the naked eye and is sometimes called the "evening star" or "morning star." Venus is covered by thick, noxious clouds of sulphuric acid that obscure its surface. The thick layers of cloud create an extreme insulating effect (like the greenhouse effect) that radiates heat back to the surface and raises the temperature to over 425°C.

Its surface is rocky, dusty and dotted with mountains and canyons and a few volcanic hot spots. There are many lava flows. Some of the mountain ranges, including the Maxwell Mantes, are enormous. Mountains within the 870 kilometre long range can reach heights of ten kilometres (much higher than the highest mountain on Earth).

In contrast to the high mountains, about 65% of Venus is comprised of smooth plains. The atmospheric pressure on the surface of Venus is intense. If you were to stand upon Venus, you would feel the same amount of pressure as if you were 100 metres underwater!

Venus is very similar in size to Earth and has about 95% of Earth's diameter. Venus is at least 80% as massive as Earth. Gravitational force on Venus is similar to Earth. A 72 kilograms earthling would weigh about 65 kilograms on Venus.

Venus is the second closest planet to the Sun at 108 million kilometres away. When Venus and Earth are on the same side of the Sun, the two planets may come within 41 million kilometres of each other. When they are on opposite sides of the Sun, they may be as far as 261 million kilometres apart.

The atmosphere of Venus is made mostly of carbon dioxide with small amounts of water vapour and nitrogen and even smaller amounts of argon, carbon monoxide, neon, and sulphur dioxide. Venus is the hottest planet in the solar system. As previously noted, temperatures on the surface exceed 425°C. The temperature in the uppermost layer of Venus' clouds averages a cold 13°C.

1. Why is Venus called Earth's sister planet?

(a) It is close to Earth
(b) It is similar in size to Earth
(c) It is hotter than Earth
(d) Much like Earth, Venus can support life

2. What does the word "obscure" mean in the sentence, "Venus is covered by thick, noxious clouds of sulphuric acid that obscure its surface."

(a) cover (b) damage (c) extend (d) create

3. Which of the following is not a feature of Venus-surface?

(a) volcanoes (b) canyons (c) plains (d) glaciers

4. The thick clouds on Venus________.

(a) make it much colder than Earth
(b) radiate extreme heat back to the surface
(c) allow heat to escape into space
(d) make the planet very colourful

Passage V

Peru's Inca Indians first grew potatoes in the Andes in about 200 B.C. Spanish conquistadors brought potatoes to Europe and colonists brought them to America. Potatoes are fourth on the list of the world's food staples - after wheat, corn and rice. Today, Americans consume about 140 pounds of potatoes per person every year while Europeans eat twice as many.

One of our favourite ways to eat potatoes is in the form of potato chips. While Benjamin Franklin was the US ambassador to France, he went to a banquet where potatoes were prepared in 20 different ways. Thomas Jefferson, who succeeded Franklin as ambassador, brought the recipe for thick-cut, French-fried potatoes to America. He served French fries to guests at the White House in 1802 and at his home, Monticello.

On 24th August, 1853, at Moon Lake Lodge in Saratoga, New York, a native-American chef named George Crum created the first potato chips. He became angry when a Diner complained that his French fries were too thick, so he sliced the potatoes as thinly as possible, making them too thin and crisp to eat with a fork. The Diner loved them and potato chips were born. In 1860, Chef Crum opened his own restaurant and offered a basket of potato chips on every table.

In the 1950s, in Ireland, Joe "Spud" Murphy and Seamus Burke, produced the world's first seasoned crisps, cheese & onion and salt and vinegar. In the United Kingdom and Ireland, crisps are what people in the United States call potato chips, while chips refer to French Fries. Ketchup flavoured chips are popular in the Mid-East of (USA and Canada. Seaweed flavour is popular in Asia, and Mexicans like chicken flavoured. chips.

Other flavours from around the world include: paprika, pickled onion, bearnaise, meat pie, chili crab, salmon teriyaki, borscht, caesar salad, roasted sausage, firecracker lobster, roast ox, haggis and black pepper, olive and spaghetti.

1. What happened in the 1950s?
- (a) The world's first potato chips were produced
- (b) The world's first seasoned French Fries were produced
- (c) The world's first seasoned potato chips were produced
- (d) The world's first French Fries were produced

2. "Potatoes are fourth on the list of the world's food staples-after wheat, corn and rice." What does "staples" mean in the above sentence?
- (a) Important crops
- (b) Something to attach documents
- (c) Departments
- (d) Metals

3. Which one of the following is true?
- (a) Ketchup flavoured Potato Chips are most popular in America
- (b) Potato chips are only popular in America
- (c) Different flavoured potato chips are popular in different parts of the world
- (d) Potato chips are not really eaten very much in Asia

4. Europeans eat________ potatoes than Americans.
- (a) about the same amount of
- (b) more
- (c) less
- (d) The passage doesn't say

Directions (Q. Nos. 1-5) Read the following poem carefully and answer the questions that follow.

Poem

The sun descending in the west,
The evening star does shine;
The birds are silent in their nest,
And I must seek for mine.
The moon, like a flower,
In heaven's high bower,
With silent delight
Sits and smiles on the night.
Farewell, green fields and happy groves,
Where flocks have took delight:
Where lambs have nibbled, silent moves
The feet of angels bright;
Unseen they pour blessing,
And joy without ceasing,
On each bud and blossom,
And each sleeping bosom.
They look in every thoughtless nest,
Where birds are covered warm;
They visit caves of every beast,
To keep them all from harm.
If they see any weeping
That should have been sleeping,
They pour sleep on their head,
And sit down by their bed.

1. The evening star rises when ....
- (a) the birds leave their nests
- (b) it is midnight
- (c) it is dawn
- (d) the sun descends in the west

2. The poet compares Moon to ....
- (a) a flower
- (b) a bird in the nest
- (c) an evening star
- (d) an angel

3. In this poem, 'bower' represents ....
- (a) a potted plant
- (b) a framework that supports climbing plants
- (c) a bouquet of flowers
- (d) a flower vase

4. The meaning of the word 'nibbled' used in the 3rd stanza of the poem is ....
- (a) eaten a small quantity
- (b) taken a small bite
- (c) taken a mouthful
- (d) tasted

5. The nest is described as 'thoughtless' because ....
- (a) the angels are blessing the birds to be happy
- (b) the birds are covered in the warmth of their nest
- (c) it is made without any thought
- (d) the occupants are asleep without any worry

Practice Set 1

A Whole Content Based Test for Class 5th English Olympiad

Directions (Q. Nos. 1-5) Read the passage carefully and select the option that you consider the most appropriate answer.

The most beautiful humming birds are found in the West Indies and South America. The crest of the tiny head of one of these shines like a sparkling crown of coloured light. The shades of colour that adorn its breast are equally brilliant. As the bird flits from one object to another, it looks more like a bright flash of sunlight than it does like a living being.

But, you ask, why are they called humming birds? It is because they make a soft, humming noise by the rapid motion of their wings — a motion so rapid, that as they fly, you can hardly see that they have wings.

One day when walking in the woods, I found the nest of one of the smallest humming birds. It was about half the size of a very small hen's egg and it was attached to a twig no thicker than a steel knitting needle. It seemed to have been made of cotton fibres and was covered with the softest bits of leaf and bark. It had two eggs in it and each was about as large as a small sugarplum.

When you approach the spot where one of these birds has built its nest, it is necessary to be careful. The mother bird will dart at you and try to peck your eyes. Its sharp beak may hurt your eyes most severely and even destroy your sight. The poor little thing knows no other way of defending its young and instinct teaches it that you might carry off its nest if you find it.

1. A humming bird's crest shines like a ....
(a) diamond
(b) gold
(c) sparkling crown of coloured light
(d) silver

2. Choose the correct statement.
(a) The humming bird looks like a black cloud
(b) The humming bird looks more like a bright flash of sunlight
(c) The humming bird looks as colourful as a dancing peacock
(d) The humming bird looks very clumsy while flying

3. This bird is called 'humming bird' because ....
(a) it is always singing
(b) it makes a humming sound while feeding its children
(c) it makes a humming noise by the rapid motion of its wings
(d) it creates humming sound while hatching its eggs

4. The idiom 'carry off' used in the last paragraph means
(a) make the planned event successful
(b) steal
(c) borrow
(d) take away

5. The antonym of the word 'approach' used in the last paragraph will be
(a) access (b) avenue (c) leave (d) advance

Directions (Q. Nos. 6-7) Fill in the blanks with suitable word from the options.

6. I don't have much ...., just two small bags.
(a) furniture (b) trolley (c) luggage (d) room

7. The use of .... should be strictly prohibited in schools.
(a) books (b) computers
(c) mobiles (d) music

Directions (Q. Nos. 8-9) Fill in the blank with the correct tense of the verb by selecting the best option.

8. The beautiful bungalow .... to a wealthy but eccentric man.
(a) is belonged (b) been belonged
(c) has belonging (d) belongs

9. My mother............ Dad's dinner in the microwave when he came back from office.
(a) has heating (b) heated
(c) is heats (d) did heating

Directions (Q. Nos. 10-11) Fill in the blanks by choosing suitable adjectives from the options.

10. The weather forecast said there would be .... rains today.
(a) heavy (b) more heavier
(c) heaviest (d) None of these

11. Take plenty of exercise to keep your body ....
(a) healthful (b) healthy (c) active (d) strong

Directions (Q. Nos. 12-13) Fill in the gaps by choosing appropriate prepositions from the options.

12. Helen is swimming .... the pool.
(a) over (b) in (c) below (d) above

13. There are special containers for transporting goods .... rail.
(a) in (b) from (c) by (d) with

Directions (Q. Nos. 14-15) Use a suitable connector in the blank and form a meaningful sentence.

14. Send us the information on a postcard .... by courier.
(a) and (b) or (c) but (d) so

15. I had planned to fly to Mauritius .... in the end I could not make it.
(a) so (b) and (c) or (d) but

Directions (Q. Nos. 16-17) Change the following sentences into passive voice so that they express the same idea. Choose from the options.

16. Who taught you such things?
(a) Who was you taught such things by?
(b) She was taught such things by who?
(c) By whom you were taught such things?
(d) By whom were you taught such things?

17. A stone struck me on the head.
(a) I was struck on a stone by the head
(b) My head was struck by a stone
(c) I had been struck by a stone on the head
(d) I was struck on the head by a stone

Directions (Q. Nos. 18-19) Change the following sentences as directed. Choose from the options.

18. The noisy family shouted, " We have won a lottery!" (Change into indirect speech)
(a) The noisy family said that they have won a lottery
(b) The noisy family exclaimed that they had won a lottery
(c) The noisy family told that they are winning a lottery
(d) The noisy family told every one that they would win a lottery.

19. The teacher ordered the boys to be quiet and do their class-work. (Change into Direct Speech)
(a) The teacher requested, "Boys, be quiet and do your class-work"
(b) The teacher said, "Be quiet, boys and do your class-work"
(c) The teacher said, "Can you please be quiet boys and do your class-work"?
(d) The teacher said, "Boys do your class work and be quiet"

Directions (Q. Nos. 20-21) Choose the synonym for the underlined word in the sentences.

20. The mother overruled her son's demand for a motorbike.
(a) neglected (b) disallowed
(c) ignored (d) fulfilled

21. The story is too fantastic to be credible.
(a) praiseworthy (b) readable
(c) false (d) believable

Directions (Q. Nos. 22-23) Choose the antonym of the underlined word in the sentences.

22. The flight was delayed because of bad weather.
(a) quickened
(b) released
(c) expedited
(d) triggered

23. The thief confessed at the police station that he had stolen my bag.
(a) consented
(b) concealed
(c) disapproved
(d) denied

Directions (Q. Nos. 24-25) Given below are four words. Three are similar in nature but one is different. Choose the odd one out.

24. (a) gloves (b) socks
(c) stockings (d) raincoat

25. (a) harmonium (b) guitar
(c) flute (d) piano

Directions (Q. Nos. 26-27) Choose the correctly punctuated sentence from the options.

26. (a) Mary shouted did you plan a tour to Mumbai last year
(b) Mary asked, "Did you plan a tour to Mumbai last year"
(c) Mary asked, "Did you plan a tour to Mumbai last year?"
(d) Mary asked, "Did you plan a tour to Mumbai last year."

27. (a) Our Prime Minister Mr Narendra Modi is visiting many foreign countries these days.
(b) Our Prime Minister, Mr Narendra Modi, is visiting many foreign countries these days.
(c) Our Prime Minister Mr Narendra Modi is visiting many foreign countries these day!
(d) Our Prime Minister Mr Narendra Modi, is visiting many foreign countries these days?

Directions (Q. Nos. 28-29) Given below are words in a jumbled manner. Rearrange them to form a meaningful sentence. Choose from the options.

28. introduce / I'd / our / to / like / you / to / Meena / cook / new
(a) I'd introduce you to like our new cook Meena
(b) I'd like you to introduce our new cook Meena
(c) I'd like to introduce you to our new cook Meena
(d) I'd like to introduce our new cook Meena to you.

29. to / again / we / seeing / forward / you / look
(a) We look again forward seeing you
(b) We look forward to seeing you again
(c) We seeing forward to look you again
(d) We look forward seeing to you again

Directions (Q. Nos. 30-31) Fill in the blank by choosing the correct word from the options.

30. The Principal .... the students on their performance.
(a) complemented (b) compleemented
(c) complimented (d) complimanted

31. Snoopy, our dog, is very naughty and often .... the furniture.
(a) choose
(b) chose
(c) chews
(d) choice

Directions (Q. Nos. 32-35) Given below is a telephonic conversation between Venkat and his sister. Based on this is given a message with some blanks. Fill in the blanks from the options given.

Venkat : Can I speak to mom?

Veena : She has gone out.

Venkat : I have to leave for Durgapur tomorrow at 4 a.m. for an Inter-School Football Match. Please ask, her to get my bag packed, as I will be back home late in the evening after practice.

Veena: I will.

Veena is going out for tuition so she writes a message.

6th July, 2015
2:30 p.m.
.......(32).......,
Venkat called up to inform that he has to leave for ....(33)....... tomorrow at 4 a.m. for an ....(34)....... as he will return home late in the evening after practice. You are requested to ......(35)...... .

Veena

32. (a) Dad (b) Mom
(c) Nani (d) Sister

33. (a) Mumbai
(b) Patna
(c) Bhagalpur
(d) Durgapur

34. (a) Inter-college match
(b) Inter-school hockey match
(c) Inter-school football match
(d) Inter-college debate

35. (a) pack his lunch
(b) pack his clothes
(c) pack his bag
(d) pack his suitcase

Directions (Q. Nos. 36-43) A letter is given below with some parts missing but substituted by boxes with number 36 to 43. Identify the missing parts. Choose from the options.

132, Sahib Building,
Ajmer,
Rajasthan
6th July, 2015

Dear Mihir

Your class teacher called me yesterday. She told me that you ....(36)....... . I was very glad to hear it. But she told me that you have become a computer addict and do not ....(37)....... in the evening. It is not good. It will ....(38)....... your health adversely.

I suggest you to ....(39)....... games. To be glued to the computer all the time is not ....(40)....... . It will affect your health as well as energy. Play any game for at least one hour. It ....(41)....... and keep you physically fit. This will also help you in your studies. Always remember the saying "work while you ....(42)....... and play while you ....(43)......., that is the way to be happy."

With Love
Jackie

36. (a) were doing well in studies
(b) are doing well in studies
(c) are good in studies
(d) are not doing well in your studies

37. (a) go out (b) have any hobby
(c) play any games (d) do any thing else

38. (a) effect (b) affect (c) harm (d) damage

39. (a) take part in evening
(b) participate in school
(c) go out and play
(d) pay attention of playing

40. (a) healthy (b) good
(c) constructive (d) energisting

41. (a) will keep you refreshed
(b) will refresh your mind
(c) will make you energised
(d) will activate you

42. (a) study (b) play (c) work (d) sleep

43. (a) study (b) play (c) sleep (d) eat

Directions (Q. Nos. 44-50) A short story is given with numbered blanks in between. Choose the option which fills the gap and makes sentence meaningful.

One evening a rich farmer was crossing a ....(44)....... flowing river on a rowboat to reach his home. He had just sold his produce at the market town ....(45)....... the river from his village.

.......(46)....... the boat reached the middle of the river, it suddenly capsized due to the swift current. The farmer panicked, because he could not swim. But just then, another boat was crossing the river near where he had fallen. The farmer begged the boatman of this boat to save him from drowning, promising all the land he ....(47)....... as a reward. Seeing the predicament of the farmer, the boatman saved him and they continued together.

After they went a ....(48)....... distance, the farmer changed his offer to half of his land, as he said the rest of the land would be a bare ....(49)....... to shield him from his wife's rebuke. As they neared the other bank of the river, the farmer reduced his offer to one-fourth of his land, saying that he required some land for himself.

When they reached the shore safely, the farmer reasoned that what could be the use of the land to a boatman who ....(50)....... most of his time on the river. So, finally he gave the boatman a reward of a five-rupee coin.

44. (a) rapid (b) deep (c) speed (d) fast

45. (a) behind (b) across
(c) through (d) by

46. (a) Because (b) Therefore
(c) As soon as (d) Thereafter

47. (a) have (b) has
(c) had (d) None of these

48. (a) little (b) few (c) some (d) very

49. (a) necessary (b) necessarily
(c) necessaries (d) necessity

50. (a) have spend (b) has spend
(c) spends (d) spending

Practice Set 2

A Whole Content Based Test for Class 5th English Olympiad

Directions (Q. Nos. 1-5) Read the passage given below carefully and select the option that you consider the most appropriate answer.

Gold is the world's greatest treasure. People use it as money and wear it as jewellery. People and countries with lots of gold are considered rich and powerful. That is why monarchs wear golden crowns and important buildings have golden domes. Being a rare commodity, gold is valuable these days. Gold is a soft yellow metal. It is found throughout Earth in tiny amounts mixed with other rocks and minerals.

Gold is one of the least reactive metals. This means that compared to copper, silver and iron, it is less likely to react with the oxygen in the air. Copper turns green over time, silver turns black and iron rusts. Gold maintains its shine even after years of use. Even gold buried underground or underwater does not lose its value or <u>lustre</u>.

Gold is measured in units called carats. Pure gold is 24 carat gold. Each country sets its own standard for gold jewellery.

For thousands of years, gold has been used for money. Gold coins were common throughout the world at one time. Gold coins were used in Britain as far back as early AD 800. In the past, Asian rulers used gold more as jewellery and a form of decoration rather than currency. They traded spices, silk and tea for Europe's gold. Today, much of the world's gold is stored as gold bars. Most countries keep a supply of gold bars that they can use to trade with other nations. This gold proves their wealth.

Today, it is a common practice in countries like India for personal wealth to be displayed by the gold they <u>adorn</u>. Indian women are known to take great pride in their collection.

1. Gold is considered to be valuable as it is ______ .

(a) is uncommon
(b) a rare commodity
(c) can be used as jewellery
(d) very expensive

2. The most special fact about gold is that ______ .

(a) it may lose its shine after a period
(b) it turns black after a few day's use
(c) it can remain in its original state for a very long period of time
(d) it can be measured in carats

3. The unit of measurement for gold is called ______ .

(a) mole (b) grain (c) gram (d) carat

4. The synonym of the word 'lustre' used in second paragraph of the passage will be _____ .

(a) dullness (b) polish
(c) brightness (d) darkness

5. The antonym of the word 'adorn' used in the last paragraph will be _____ .

(a) furnish (b) beautify
(c) deform (d) enhance

Directions (Q. Nos. 6-7) Fill in the blanks with suitable nouns.

6. Nivedita reads news on television. She is a _____ .

(a) proof reader (b) publisher
(c) news reader (d) editor

7. John draws the designs of buildings. He is a/an ______ .

(a) jeweller (b) librarian
(c) astronaut (d) architect

Directions (Q. Nos. 8-9) Find the odd one out.

8. (a) hut (b) cottage
(c) hutch (d) house

9. (a) cobbler (b) sailor
(c) traitor (d) watchman

Directions (Q. Nos. 10-11) Choose the correct verb to fill in the blanks.

10. The white shirt and the black trousers .... dirty.

(a) was (b) were (c) has (d) is

11. The children .... trees in the school.

(a) has planting (b) is planting
(c) are planting (d) have planting

Directions (Q. Nos. 12-13) Fill in the blank by choosing the appropriate article from the options.

12. He knows what honour is but that does not make him .... honourable man.

(a) an (b) the (c) a (d) this

13. As, I was walking back from school, I saw .... most unusual thing.

(a) a (b) that (c) an (d) the

Directions (Q. Nos. 14-15) Choose suitable conjunction to fill the blanks.

14. .... I have had my lunch, I can still eat a pizza.

(a) However (b) Moreover
(c) Although (d) Already

15. I am not feeling well, ... I will come to the party.

(a) because (b) since
(c) unless (d) but

Directions (Q. Nos. 16-17) Choose suitable preposition to fill the blanks.

16. Because we have no cars, we go everywhere .... foot.

(a) with (b) for (c) by (d) on

17. The pied piper stepped .... the street.

(a) over (b) into (c) under (d) upto

Directions (Q. Nos. 18-19) Change the voice of following sentences as directed.

18. They are building a house next door to our school (change into passive voice).

(a) A house next door to our school is being built by them.
(b) Next door to our school is being built a house by them.
(c) A house next door to our school is being built by them.
(d) A house is being built next door by them to our school.

19. Independence day was celebrated by the residents. (Change into Active Voice)

(a) The residents are celebrating Independence day.
(b) The residents celebrate Independence day.
(c) The residents celebrated Independence day.
(d) The residents have been celebrating Independence day.

Directions (Q. Nos. 20-21) Choose the correct synonym of the underlined phrase from the options.

20. I am busy, <u>hold on</u> for a minute.

(a) stay (b) wait
(c) remain (d) linger

21. After a long journey of 23 hours, he was completely <u>worn out</u>.

(a) sickened (b) exhausted
(c) frail (d) sleepy

Directions (Q. Nos. 22-23) Choose the word that is most nearly opposite in meaning to the given word.

22. Solitary

(a) Friendly (b) Isolated
(c) Together (d) Lonely

23. Consent

(a) Discard (b) Surrender
(c) Approve (d) dissent

Directions (Q. Nos. 24-25) Choose appropriate word from the options to complete the sentence.

24. Your are in a .... when you are forced to choose between two unpleasant options.

(a) confusion (b) crisis
(c) impatience (d) dilemma

25. When it does not rain properly people face ....

(a) shortage (b) prosperity
(c) famine (d) poverty

Directions (Q. Nos. 26-27) Select the option which is punctuated correctly.

26. (a) We'll need a board counters and a pair of dice.
(b) We'll need a board, counters and a pair of dice.
(c) We'll need a board, counters and, a pair of dice.
(d) We'll need, a board, counters and a pair of dice.

27. (a) Sam asked, "Have I time to get popcorn", after he had bought his ticket.
(b) Sam asked, "Have I time to get popcorns?
(c) Sam asked, "Have I time to get popcorns?" after he had bought his ticket.
(d) Sam asked "have I time to get popcorns"! after he had bought his ticket.

Directions (Q. Nos. 28-29) Each question consists of two words which have a certain relationship to each other followed by four pairs of words. Select the most appropriate pair having the same relationship as the given pair.

28. Sight : Blind
(a) Language : Deaf
(b) Voice : Vibration
(c) Speech : Dumb
(d) Tongue : Sound

29. Distance : Kilometre
(a) Weight : Scale
(b) Present : Past
(c) Liquid : Litre
(d) Fame : Television

Directions (Q. Nos. 30-31) Fill the blanks by choosing the most suitable option.

30. arrival : departure : : .... : death
(a) person
(b) birth
(c) life
(d) train

31. Car : Road : : Train ....
(a) vehicle
(b) airstrip
(c) wheel
(d) track

Directions (Q. Nos. 32-33) Given below are words in a jumbled order. Rearrange them to make a proper sentence and select the correct option.

32. the / onions / chopping / the / in / kitchen / is / Shilpa
(a) In the kitchen Shilpa is onion chopping
(b) Shilpa is chopping the onions in the kitchen
(c) Chopping the onions Shilpa is in the kitchen
(d) The onions chopping in the kitchen Shilpa is

33. a / come / has / long / certainly / women's / tennis / way
(a) Certainly women's tennis has a long way come
(b) Women's tennis a long way has certainly come
(c) Women's tennis has certainly come a long way
(d) A long way women's tennis has come certainly

Directions (Q. Nos. 34-38) Given below is an application by Anil Mehta to the school Principal to issue him a school leaving certificate as his father has been posted out of Delhi. Complete it by filling the blanks with the most suitable option given below.

The Principal
Navodaya School,
Lodhi Road,
New Delhi
8th July, 2015
Subject: ....(34).......
Respected Sir,
This is to ....(35)....... you that my father is in a government job and has been ....(36)....... to Arunachal Pradesh. Thus, I will not be able ....(37)....... my studies in this school. Kindly issue me a ....(38)........ .
Thanking you
Respectfully yours
Anil Mehta, Class V-B

34. (a) Issue of certificate
(b) Request for school leaving certificate
(c) Permission to leave the school
(d) Allow to leave

35. (a) inform
(b) tell
(c) put before
(d) intimate

36. (a) sent away
(b) flown
(c) transferred
(d) gone

37. (a) to study here
(b) to continue
(c) to pursue
(d) to carry on

38. (a) school leaving certificate
(b) permission to leave school
(c) leaving certificate
(d) freeship certificate

Directions (Q. No. 39) Rearrange the words given below to form a meaningful sentence, selecting the correct sentence from the options given.

39. reached/the/the/after/they/theatre/had/begun/show
(a) The show had begun after they reached the theatre
(b) They reached the theatre after the show had begun
(c) Show after the theatre had begun they reached the
(d) Begun the show after they had reached the theatre

40. Fill in the blank with an appropriate adverb from the options given.

The soldiers fought______ though the conditions were unbearable.

(a) courageously
(b) sadly
(c) hardly
(d) fortunately

Directions (Q. Nos. 41-42) Fill in the blank with the correct tense of the verb by selecting the best option.

41. Rajendra_______ eating momos and burgers.

(a) enjoys
(b) is enjoy
(c) had enjoying
(d) will enjoying

42. Ratnesh______ that you_____ .

(a) will think, mistake
(b) thought, mistook
(c) think, mistake
(d) thinks, are mistaken

43. Fill in the blank with the correct pronoun to complete the sentence given.

We decided to approach the Principal____ as our teacher did not do so.

(a) myself (b) ourselves
(c) themselves (d) ourself

44. Choose the right modal verb from the options given to fill in the blank.

Dalbir couldn't find his purse. He thought he_____ it somewhere on the way.

(a) drop (b) was dropping
(c) may have dropped (d) must dropped

Directions (Q. No. 45) Choose the option which means nearly the same as idiom underlined in the sentence given below.

45. He was always a black sheep in the community due to his intoxication with drugs.

(a) A person who causes shame or embarrassment
(b) Owner of a black coloured sheep
(c) Dark-skinned person
(d) Most virtuous character

Directions (Q. Nos. 46-50) Given below is a telephonic conversation between Kanu and Charu. Based on this is message has been written by Kanu. Fill in the blanks from the option given.

Kanu : This is Kanu. May I know who is calling?
Charu : Hello, Kanu. This is Charu here. Is Bhavna at home?
Kanu : No, Charu, Bhavna has gone to her friend's house. She will be back after an hour or so.
Charu : All right; when she comes back, please tell her that I am going to Rehana's birthday party this evening. If Bhavna wants to go there, please tell her to be ready by 5:30 pm. I will pick her up.
Kanu : Don't worry. I'll convey the message. Anything else?
Charu : No thanks, bye.

Kanu is going out, so she writes a message for Bhavna

.......(46).......
14th July, 2015
3:30 p.m.
Bhavna,
Your friend Charu called up ....(47)....... you that she is going to ....(48)....... this evening. She asked you ....49....... by 5:30 pm if you want to go. She will ....(50)........
Kanu

46. (a) Appeal (b) Notice
(c) Message (d) E-mail

47. (a) telling (b) to inform
(c) to enquire (d) to request

48. (a) her friend's house
(b) watch a movie
(c) Rehana's birthday party
(d) farewell party

49. (a) to get ready
(b) to buy some gifts
(c) to give her money
(d) to be ready

50. (a) escort you (b) take you
(c) call you (d) pick you up

1 Nouns

1. (c) **2.** (d) **3.** (d) **4.** (b) **5.** (b) **6.** (b) **7.** (c) **8.** (b) **9.** (d) **10.** (b)
11. (b) **12.** (c) **13.** (a) **14.** (c) **15.** (c) **16.** (b) **17.** (b) **18.** (d) **19.** (b) **20.** (d)
21. (d) **22.** (b) **23.** (c) **24.** (d) **25.** (c) **26.** (b) **27.** (d) **28.** (d) **29.** (d) **30.** (b)
31. (b) **32.** (d) **33.** (c) **34.** (a) **35.** (c) **36.** (d) **37.** (b) **38.** (c) **39.** (c) **40.** (a)
41. (b) **42.** (d) **43.** (b) **44.** (b) **45.** (b) **46.** (c) **47.** (c) **48.** (a) **49.** (c) **50.** (b)

2 Pronouns

1. (d) **2.** (d) **3.** (a) **4.** (d) **5.** (c) **6.** (b) **7.** (c) **8.** (d) **9.** (b) **10.** (c)
11. (c) **12.** (b) **13.** (b) **14.** (d) **15.** (d) **16.** (b) **17.** (d) **18.** (b) **19.** (b) **20.** (b)
21. (c) **22.** (d) **23.** (c) **24.** (b) **25.** (d) **26.** (d) **27.** (a) **28.** (c) **29.** (c) **30.** (b)
31. (b) **32.** (c) **33.** (d) **34.** (d) **35.** (b) **36.** (c) **37.** (a) **38.** (b) **39.** (c) **40.** (b)
41. (d) **42.** (d) **43.** (b) **44.** (c) **45.** (c) **46.** (b) **47.** (b) **48.** (c) **49.** (b) **50.** (b)
51. (d) **52.** (a)

3 Articles

1. (a) **2.** (c) **3.** (b) **4.** (c) **5.** (d) **6.** (c) **7.** (d) **8.** (d) **9.** (a) **10.** (c)
11. (b) **12.** (a) **13.** (b) **14.** (d) **15.** (b) **16.** (d) **17.** (b) **18.** (b **19.** (c) **20.** (d)
21. (c) **22.** (b) **23.** (c) **24.** (a) **25.** (d) **26.** (d) **27.** (a) **28.** (c) **29.** (a) **30.** (a)
31. (b) **32.** (c) **33.** (d) **34.** (c) **35.** (b) **36.** (b) **37.** (b) **38.** (b) **39.** (b) **40.** (b)
41. (b) **42.** (c) **43.** (c) **44.** (c)

4 Adjectives

1. (c) **2.** (b) **3.** (c) **4.** (c) **5.** (b) **6.** (d) **7.** (d) **8.** (b) **9.** (b) **10.** (d)
11. (c) **12.** (b) **13.** (b) **14.** (b) **15.** (b) **16.** (b) **17.** (a) **18.** (c) **19.** (d) **20.** (c)
21. (b) **22.** (c) **23.** (b) **24.** (c) **25.** (b) **26.** (c) **27.** (b) **28.** (c) **29.** (c) **30.** (c)
31. (a) **32.** (b) **33.** (a) **34.** (d) **35.** (b) **36.** (c) **37.** (d) **38.** (d) **39.** (b) **40.** (c)
41. (c) **42.** (b) **43.** (b) **44.** (c) **45.** (a) **46.** (b) **47.** (c) **48.** (c) **49.** (a) **50.** (c)

5 Verbs

1. (b) **2.** (b) **3.** (c) **4.** (c) **5.** (c) **6.** (a) **7.** (a) **8.** (d) **9.** (a) **10.** (c)
11. (d) **12.** (d) **13.** (d) **14.** (d) **15.** (b) **16.** (b) **17.** (c) **18.** (b) **19.** (b) **20.** (b)
21. (d) **22.** (d) **23.** (d) **24.** (b) **25.** (c) **26.** (a) **27.** (b) **28.** (b) **29.** (c) **30.** (c)
31. (a) **32.** (c) **33.** (a) **34.** (c) **35.** (b) **36.** (b) **37.** (c) **38.** (d) **39.** (c) **40.** (c)
41. (b) **42.** (b) **43.** (a) **44.** (b) **45.** (c) **46.** (b) **47.** (a) **48.** (b) **49.** (c) **50.** (a)
51. (a)

6 Tenses

1. (c) **2.** (d) **3.** (c) **4.** (b) **5.** (b) **6.** (b) **7.** (c) **8.** (a) **9.** (c) **10.** (b)
11. (c) **12.** (a) **13.** (b) **14.** (a) **15.** (a) **16.** (c) **17.** (c) **18.** (b) **19.** (d) **20.** (c)
21. (a) **22.** (c) **23.** (a) **24.** (c) **25.** (b) **26.** (c) **27.** (c) **28.** (a) **29.** (c) **30.** (c)
31. (a) **32.** (b) **33.** (b) **34.** (b) **35.** (b) **36.** (c) **37.** (a) **38.** (a) **39.** (c) **40.** (a)
41. (b) **42.** (a) **43.** (c) **44.** (b) **45.** (c) **46.** (a) **47.** (b) **48.** (b) **49.** (a) **50.** (d)

7 Prepositions

1. (c)	2. (c)	3. (b)	4. (c)	5. (b)	6. (b)	7. (b)	8. (b)	9. (b)	10. (a)
11. (c)	12. (d)	13. (d)	14. (b)	15. (b)	16. (a)	17. (c)	18. (b)	19. (c)	20. (b)
21. (d)	22. (a)	23. (a)	24. (c)	25. (d)	26. (b)	27. (c)	28. (a)	29. (b)	30. (b)
31. (b)	32. (c)	33. (b)	34. (c)	35. (a)	36. (b)	37. (c)	38. (c)	39. (a)	40. (b)
41. (c)	42. (b)	43. (a)	44. (b)	45. (a)	46. (c)	47. (b)	48. (a)	49. (b)	50. (a)

8 Conjunctions

1. (d)	2. (b)	3. (d)	4. (c)	5. (d)	6. (c)	7. (d)	8. (c)	9. (a)	10. (a)
11. (c)	12. (c)	13. (b)	14. (b)	15. (c)	16. (d)	17. (b)	18. (d)	19. (b)	20. (a)
21. (d)	22. (d)	23. (d)	24. (c)	25. (a)	26. (d)	27. (c)	28. (c)	29. (a)	30. (b)
31. (c)	32. (c)	33. (c)	34. (b)	35. (c)	36. (c)	37. (c)	38. (b)	39. (c)	40. (b)
41. (c)	42. (c)	43. (c)	44. (a)	45. (b)	46. (b)	47. (c)			

9 Punctuation

1. (d)	2. (c)	3. (a)	4. (b)	5. (d)	6. (c)	7. (a)	8. (c)	9. (c)	10. (b)
11. (a)	12. (b)	13. (d)	14. (b)	15. (c)	16. (d)	17. (b)	18. (c)	19. (d)	20. (b)
21. (a)	22. (c)	23. (d)	24. (c)	25. (c)	26. (b)	27. (b)	28. (d)	29. (a)	30. (c)
31. (c)	32. (c)	33. (b)	34. (a)	35. (b)	36. (b)	37. (c)	38. (a)	39. (a)	40. (a)
41. (a)	42. (d)	43. (b)	44. (c)	45. (d)					

10 Active and Passive Voice

1. (c)	2. (b)	3. (b)	4. (a)	5. (c)	6. (c)	7. (a)	8. (c)	9. (d)	10. (b)
11. (c)	12. (a)	13. (c)	14. (d)	15. (c)	16. (d)	17. (d)	18. (b)	19. (a)	20. (c)
21. (a)	22. (b)	23. (c)	24. (c)	25. (a)	26. (b)	27. (c)	28. (d)	29. (c)	30. (b)
31. (a)	32. (b)	33. (a)	34. (d)	35. (c)	36. (d)	37. (d)	38. (b)	39. (a)	40. (a)
41. (a)	42. (d)	43. (c)	44. (b)	45. (a)	46. (c)	47. (c)	48. (a)	49. (b)	50. (d)

11 Vocabulary

1. (d)	2. (c)	3. (b)	4. (c)	5. (b)	6. (b)	7. (d)	8. (c)	9. (c)	10. (d)
11. (c)	12. (a)	13. (d)	14. (d)	15. (c)	16. (b)	17. (a)	18. (a)	19. (c)	20. (c)
21. (c)	22. (a)	23. (b)	24. (b)	25. (d)	26. (a)	27. (a)	28. (a)	29. (c)	30. (a)
31. (d)	32. (c)	33. (b)	34. (d)	35. (d)	36. (c)	37. (b)	38. (b)	39. (c)	40. (b)
41. (c)	42. (b)	43. (c)	44. (c)						

12 Jumbled Words and Jumbled Sentences

1. TOMORROW	2. HOLIDAY	3. LIBRARY	4. FOOTBALL	5. KITCHEN		
6. CHICKEN	7. BOARD	8. COMPUTER	9. DOCTOR	10. CIRCUS		
11. (b)	12. (c)	13. (c)	14. (b)	15. (d)	16. (b)	17. (c)
18. (a)	19. (c)	20. (b)	21. (b)	22. (c)	23. (a)	24. (b)
25. (b)	26. (c)	27. (b)	28. (c)	29. (b)	30. (c)	31. (b)
32. (c)	33. (d)	34. (a)	35. (d)	36. (c)	37. (c)	38. (c)
39. (b)	40. (d)	41. (a)	42. (d)	43. (d)	44. (b)	45. (c)
46. (c)	47. (a)	48. (a)	49. (d)	50. (c)		

13 Synonyms

1. (b)	**2.** (c)	**3.** (b)	**4.** (a)	**5.** (d)	**6.** (a)	**7.** (d)	**8.** (b)	**9.** (c)	**10.** (d)
11. (b)	**12.** (c)	**13.** (b)	**14.** (b)	**15.** (c)	**16.** (c)	**17.** (a)	**18.** (c)	**19.** (c)	**20.** (a)
21. (c)	**22.** (b)	**23.** (c)	**24.** (b)	**25.** (b)	**26.** (b)	**27.** (c)	**28.** (c)	**29.** (b)	**30.** (d)
31. (c)	**32.** (c)	**33.** (b)	**34.** (b)	**35.** (a)	**36.** (d)	**37.** (c)	**38.** (b)	**39.** (b)	**40.** (c)
41. (c)	**42.** (b)	**43.** (d)	**44.** (b)	**45.** (b)					

14 Antonyms

1. (c)	**2.** (c)	**3.** (a)	**4.** (b)	**5.** (c)	**6.** (d)	**7.** (d)	**8.** (c)	**9.** (b)	**10.** (c)
11. (d)	**12.** (c)	**13.** (a)	**14.** (c)	**15.** (b)	**16.** (d)	**17.** (c)	**18.** (b)	**19.** (d)	**20.** (b)
21. (d)	**22.** (d)	**23.** (b)	**24.** (c)	**25.** (d)	**26.** (a)	**27.** (d)	**28.** (b)	**29.** (c)	**30.** (d)
31. (c)	**32.** (b)	**33.** (d)	**34.** (b)	**35.** (c)	**36.** (c)	**37.** (b)	**38.** (b)	**39.** (b)	**40.** (c)
41. (b)	**42.** (a)	**43.** (c)	**44.** (d)	**45.** (c)	**46.** (d)	**47.** (d)	**48.** (c)	**49.** (a)	**50.** (a)

15 Short Composition

1. (c)	**2.** (d)	**3.** (a)	**4.** (b)	**5.** (b)	**6.** (a)	**7.** (a)	**8.** (b)	**9.** (c)	**10.** (a)
11. (c)	**12.** (d)	**13.** (b)	**14.** (d)	**15.** (c)	**16.** (c)	**17.** (d)	**18.** (c)	**19.** (c)	**20.** (a)
21. (c)	**22.** (b)	**23.** (c)	**24.** (c)	**25.** (d)	**26.** (b)	**27.** (c)	**28.** (b)	**29.** (b)	**30.** (b)
31. (d)	**32.** (b)	**33.** (a)	**34.** (c)	**35.** (b)	**36.** (c)	**37.** (b)			

16 Reading Comprehension

Passage I

1. (c) **2.** (d) **3.** (c) **4.** (a) **5.** (b)

Passage II

1. (c) **2.** (d) **3.** (b) **4.** (c) **5.** (b)

Passage III

1. (b) **2.** (a) **3.** (b) **4.** (b) **5.** (c)

Passage IV

1. (b) **2.** (a) **3.** (d) **4.** (b)

Passage V

1. (c) **2.** (a) **3.** (c) **4.** (b)

Poem

1. (d) **2.** (a) **3.** (c) **4.** (b) **5.** (d)

Practice Set 1

1.	(c)	**2.**	(b)	**3.**	(c)	**4.**	(d)	**5.**	(c)	**6.**	(c)	**7.**	(c)	**8.**	(d)	**9.**	(b)	**10.**	(a)
11.	(b)	**12.**	(b)	**13.**	(c)	**14.**	(b)	**15.**	(d)	**16.**	(d)	**17.**	(d)	**18.**	(b)	**19.**	(b)	**20.**	(b)
21.	(d)	**22.**	(c)	**23.**	(d)	**24.**	(d)	**25.**	(c)	**26.**	(c)	**27.**	(b)	**28.**	(c)	**29.**	(b)	**30.**	(c)
31.	(c)	**32.**	(b)	**33.**	(d)	**34.**	(c)	**35.**	(c)	**36.**	(b)	**37.**	(c)	**38.**	(b)	**39.**	(c)	**40.**	(b)
41.	(b)	**42.**	(c)	**43.**	(b)	**44.**	(d)	**45.**	(b)	**46.**	(c)	**47.**	(c)	**48.**	(a)	**49.**	(d)	**50.**	(c)

Practice Set 2

1.	(b)	**2.**	(c)	**3.**	(d)	**4.**	(c)	**5.**	(c)	**6.**	(c)	**7.**	(d)	**8.**	(c)	**9.**	(c)	**10.**	(b)
11.	(c)	**12.**	(a)	**13.**	(d)	**14.**	(c)	**15.**	(d)	**16.**	(d)	**17.**	(b)	**18.**	(c)	**19.**	(c)	**20.**	(b)
21.	(b)	**22.**	(c)	**23.**	(d)	**24.**	(d)	**25.**	(c)	**26.**	(b)	**27.**	(c)	**28.**	(c)	**29.**	(c)	**30.**	(b)
31.	(d)	**32.**	(b)	**33.**	(c)	**34.**	(b)	**35.**	(a)	**36.**	(c)	**37.**	(b)	**38.**	(a)	**39.**	(b)	**40.**	(a)
41.	(a)	**42.**	(d)	**43.**	(b)	**44.**	(c)	**45.**	(a)	**46.**	(c)	**47.**	(b)	**48.**	(c)	**49.**	(d)	**50.**	(d)

9 789352 511983

Printed by Libri Plureos GmbH in Hamburg,
Germany